CW00552619

The Environment

The Environment

BY POPE BENEDICT XVI

Collected and Edited by Jacquelyn Lindsey

Our Sunday Visitor Publishing Division
Our Sunday Visitor, Inc.
Huntington, Indiana 46750

ISBN: 978-1-61278-628-5 (Inventory No. T1325)

eISBN: 978-1-61278-220-1

LCCN: 2012932797

Interior design by M. Urgo

Cover design by Lindsey Riesen

Cover art: "Life" (oil on panel), by Rebecca Campbell (Contemporary Artist), Private Collection/Courtesy of Jonathan Cooper, Park Walk Gallery, London/The Bridgeman Art Library

PRINTED IN THE UNITED STATES OF AMERICA

TABLE OF CONTENTS

INTRODUCTION

To speak about the environment is to speak about a great deal! In this introduction to an enormously rich and inspiring collection, I would like to offer you a few suggestions for appreciating Pope Benedict XVI's teaching on environment and ecology.

Four Key Words

Environment comes from the French *virer*, "to turn" or "to veer," and *environ* "around," from which we get "to turn round" and, finally, "surroundings." In the title of this book, ***environment*** not only refers to all the surrounding conditions that influence plant and animal life, but also suggests that we pay ever more careful attention to how pollution might damage them.

Ecology starts with three letters, "eco," from the Greek *oikos*, which means "home or household"; and then adds *logos*, which is "discourse, meaning, sense." So ecology is meaningful talk about our home, the earth. The modern term "ecology" was introduced by the biologist Ernest Häckel in 1869. It is the scientific study of living beings in relationship with their surroundings. Being "a wondrous work of the Creator," the natural environment contains "a 'grammar' which sets forth ends and criteria for its wise use, not its reckless exploitation."[1]

Ecology, as treated by the Holy Father, relates to two other words beginning with more or less the same letters. ***Economy*** starts with *oikos* and adds *nomos*, "rule" or "law"; and ***ecumenical*** builds on *oikos* to become *oikoumenē gē*, "the whole inhabited world" and all its inhabitants, including our descendents. The three words beginning with *oikos* imply how we should dwell and behave here on our planet, one household common to all.

Moreover, each of the four key words suggests a quality that we need in order to embrace God's gift of nature:

> **environment** calls for *awareness*;
> **ecology** enjoins *responsibility*;
> **economy** requires *justice*; and
> **ecumenical** hearkens to *unity*, not only global, but also intergenerational.

Thus, in addition to their definitional meanings, these four key words also contain suggestive clues for appreciating this sollection. When reading Pope Benedict on the environment, please notice what should stimulate us all to heighten awareness, accept responsibility, act justly, and strive for unity.

Extremes

Concern for the environment can be led astray when notions are taken to the extreme. "Nature" contains our human family; it is neither taboo (beyond human touch) nor should it be subjected to abuse. Similarly, "nature" is not more important than "human" but equally — the "human" must not presume to have the monopoly on all meaning and design in "nature." Unfortunately there are many common distortions which lead to "attitudes of neo-paganism or a new pantheism — human salvation cannot come from nature alone, understood in a purely naturalistic sense."

"It is also necessary to reject the opposite position, which aims at total technical dominion over nature, because the natural environment is more than raw material to be manipulated at our pleasure... When nature, including the human being, is viewed as the result of mere chance or evolutionary determinism, our sense of responsibility wanes."

There can scarcely be more dramatic illustrations of such irresponsibility than the chronic social injustices that force the poor into agricultural practices which result in wanton deforestation, erosion, desertification; or the warmongering that leaves devastated landscapes in its wake. We must not ignore the obvious truth that the "deterioration of nature is in fact closely connected to the culture that shapes human coexistence.... Just as human virtues are interrelated, such that the weakening of one places others at risk, so the ecological system is based on respect for a plan that affects both the health of society and its good relationship with nature.... Our duties toward the environment are linked to our duties toward the human person, considered in himself and in relation to others. It would be wrong to uphold one set of duties while trampling on the other."

Having asked us to think clearly about the environment, the Holy Father shows us how to put order into our thinking, keeping things in their proper places, not exaggerating legitimate concerns to the point of becoming ideological and harmful. Let us do the same.

Human Ecology
If we agree that environmental language and action should avoid extremes, this raises the question: What are the proper boundaries?

In the early 1990s, Blessed John Paul II gave eloquent expression to environmental concern: "People are rightly worried — though much less than they should be — about preserving the natural habitats of the various animal species threatened with extinction, because they realize that each of these species makes its particular contribution to the balance of nature in general." He then masterfully broadened and deepened the scope: "In addition to the irrational destruction of the natural environment, we must also mention the more serious destruction of the human environment.... Too little effort is made to *safeguard the moral conditions for an authentic 'human ecology.'*"[2]

Pope Benedict goes on to develop "the links between natural ecology, or respect for nature, and human ecology. Experience shows that *disregard for the environment always harms human coexistence*, and vice versa."[3] And the vital importance of human ecology rests in this: to "protect mankind from self-destruction.... If there is a lack of respect for the right to life and to a natural death, if human conception, gestation and birth are made artificial, if human embryos are sacrificed to research, the conscience of society ends up losing the concept of human ecology and, along with it, that of environmental ecology."

Human nature (which human ecology is supposed to take care of) emerges from what has been divinely revealed. "*Nature expresses a design of love and truth.* It is prior to us, and it has been given to us by God as the setting for our life. Nature speaks to us of the Creator (cf. Rom 1:20) and his love for humanity. It is destined to be 'recapitulated' in Christ at the end of time (cf. Eph 1:9-10; Col 1:19-20). Thus it too is a 'vocation.'[4] Nature is at our disposal ... as a gift of the Creator who has given it an inbuilt order, enabling man to draw from it the principles needed in order 'to till it and keep it' (Gn 2:15)."

What is most basic, then, is "the overall moral tenor of society," and we see how it eventually but inevitably affects the health of the planet. Pope Benedict's messages on environment and ecology guide a sound understanding which consistently keeps the *human* within nature (not opposed or neglected) and gratefully acknowledges *nature* as work and gift of the Creator. What perspective could be more important than this!

Conclusion

The Holy Father accepts that, as pope, he has "an inner obligation to struggle for the preservation of the environment and to oppose the destruction of creation."[5] Our Sunday Visitor has therefore done well in making his writings on the environment available to Catholics and others who, learning from his teaching, will contribute to the Church's ministry of responsibility towards creation. With them Pope Benedict now shares his sense of mission:

> In view of the threatening catastrophe, there is the recognition everywhere that we must make moral decisions.... [But] how can the great moral will, which everybody affirms and everyone invokes, become a personal decision? For unless that happens, politics remains impotent.

> Who, therefore can ensure that this general awareness also penetrates the personal sphere? This can be done only by an authority that touches the conscience that is close to the individual and does not merely call for eye-catching events...

> [Here the Church] not only has a major responsibility; she is, I would say, often the only hope. For she is so close to people's consciences that she can move them to particular acts of self-denial and can inculcate basic attitudes in souls.[6]

After reading, meditating and reflecting, let us proceed to conversion and to action, implementing the human and environmental ecology that our global family and planetary household badly need, now and for generations to come ...

… but first and finally let us turn to prayer. "In nature, the believer recognizes the wonderful result of God's creative activity" from the beginning; and "the Christian vision of nature as the fruit of God's creation" culminates in adoration as, for example, Pierre Teilhard de Chardin in his magnificent *Hymn to Matter*:

> Blessed are you, reality ever new-born; you who, by constantly shattering our mental categories, force us to go ever further and further in our pursuit of the truth; triple abyss of stars and atoms and generations: you who, by overflowing and dissolving our narrow standards of measurement, reveal to us the dimensions of God.[7]

Cardinal Peter K.A. Turkson
President, Pontifical Council for Justice and Peace
Feast of the Annunciation, 2012

1. The several quotations from *Caritas in veritate* (Nos. 48, 51) are not referenced, but citations from other sources are footnoted.

2. John Paul II, *Centesimus Annus*, No. 38.

3. Benedict XVI, *Message*, World Day of Peace 2007, No. 8.

4. John Paul II, *Message*, World Day of Peace 1990, No. 6.

5. Benedict XVI, *Light of the World* (A Conversation with Peter Seewald), 2010, p. 20.

6. *Light of the World*, p. 45, referring to World Climate Conference in Copenhagen, December 2009.

7. Pierre Teilhard de Chardin S.J., *Hymn to the Universe*, tran. Simon Bartholomew, NY: Harper & Row, 1965, pp. 68-69.

I willingly join in spirit all who are grateful to the Lord for the fruits of the earth and the work of human hands, renewing the pressing invitation to respect the natural environment, a precious resource entrusted to our stewardship. — Pope Benedict XVI (Angelus, November 15, 2009)

EDITOR'S NOTE: With the exception of the Introduction by Cardinal Peter Turkson, the material in this book is derived from Pope Benedict XVI's audiences, speeches, encyclicals, letters, messages, and homilies. The texts have been edited only slightly to facilitate presentation in book form. Footnotes indicate date and occasion of the original presentation.

Agriculture and Dialogue[1]

The theme chosen for this day, *Agriculture and the Dialogue of Cultures*, is an invitation to consider dialogue as an effective instrument to create the conditions for food security. Dialogue requires people and nations to join forces to serve the common good. The convergence of all the protagonists, combined with effective cooperation, can help to build *true peace,* making it possible to overcome the recurrent temptations of war that stem from differences in cultural outlook, race, or level of development.

It is also important to be directly alert to human situations, with the aim of maintaining the diversity of development models and forms of technical assistance in accordance with the particular conditions of each country and each community, whether it is a matter of economic or environmental or even social, cultural, and spiritual conditions.

Technical progress will only be truly effective if it has a place in a broader perspective that centers on man and is concerned to consider all his needs and aspirations, for, as Scripture says: "Not on bread alone is man to live" (cf. Dt 8: 3; Mt 4:4). This will also enable every people to draw from its patrimony of values in order to share its material and spiritual riches for the benefit of all.

The ambitious and complex goals that your organization sets itself will not be achieved unless the protection of human dignity, the first and last of the fundamental rights, becomes the criterion that inspires and directs all its efforts.

The Catholic Church, which also participates in actions that aim at truly harmonious development, in collaboration with the partners present on the spot, hopes to encourage the FAO's activity and efforts in order to initiate a true dialogue of cultures at her level and thereby to contribute to increasing the ability to

---

1   Pope Benedict XVI, Message to the Director General of FAO (Food and Agriculture Organization of the United Nations), October 12, 2005.

nourish the world population, with respect for biodiversity. In fact, the human being must not rashly compromise the natural balance, a result of the order of creation, but, on the contrary, must take care to pass on to future generations an earth able to feed them.

In this spirit, I ask the Almighty to bless the mission of the FAO, which is so necessary, and the commitment of its directors and officials, with a view to guaranteeing to each member of the human family his or her daily bread.

We might say that Advent is the season in which Christians must rekindle in their hearts the hope that they will be able with God's help to renew the world.

In this regard I would also like to remember today the constitution of the Second Vatican Council *Gaudium et Spes,* on the Church in the Modern World: It is a text deeply imbued with Christian hope.

I am referring in particular to No. 39, entitled "New Heavens and a New Earth." In it we read: "We are taught that God is preparing a new dwelling and a new earth in which righteousness dwells (cf. 2 Cor 5:2; 2 Pt 3:13).... Far from diminishing our concern to develop this earth, the expectancy of a new earth should spur us on, for it is here that the body of a new human family grows."

Indeed, we will find the good fruits of our hard work when Christ delivers to the Father his eternal and universal Kingdom. May Mary Most Holy, Virgin of Advent, obtain that we live this time of grace in a watchful and hardworking way while we await the Lord.

---

2 Pope Benedict XVI, Angelus, November 27, 2005.

BEING A GLOBAL FAMILY[3]

"I bring you good news of a great joy ... for to you is born this day in the city of David a Savior, who is Christ the Lord" (Lk 2:10-11).

Last night we heard once more the angel's message to the shepherds, and we experienced anew the atmosphere of that holy night, Bethlehem Night, when the Son of God became man, was born in a lowly stable, and dwelt among us. On this solemn day, the angel's proclamation rings out once again, inviting us, the men and women of the third millennium, to welcome the Savior. May the people of today's world not hesitate to let him enter their homes, their cities, their nations, everywhere on earth! In the millennium just past, and especially in the last centuries, immense progress was made in the areas of technology and science. Today we can dispose of vast material resources. But the men and women in our technological age risk becoming victims of their own intellectual and technical achievements, ending up in spiritual barrenness and emptiness of heart. That is why it is so important for us to open our minds and hearts to the Birth of Christ, this event of salvation which can give new hope to the life of each human being.

"Wake up, O man! For your sake God became man" (Saint Augustine, *Sermo*, 185). Wake up, O men and women of the third millennium!

At Christmas, the Almighty becomes a child and asks for our help and protection. His way of showing that he is God challenges our way of being human. By knocking at our door, he challenges us and our freedom; he calls us to examine how we understand and live our lives. The modern age is often seen as an awakening of reason from its slumbers, humanity's enlightenment after an age of darkness. Yet without the light of Christ,

---

3 Pope Benedict XVI, *Urbi et Orbi* Message, Christmas 2005.

the light of reason is not sufficient to enlighten humanity and the world. For this reason, the words of the Christmas Gospel: "the true Light that enlightens every man was coming into this world" (Jn 1:9) resound now more than ever as a proclamation of salvation. "It is only in the mystery of the Word made flesh that the mystery of humanity truly becomes clear" (*Gaudium et Spes*, 22). The Church does not tire of repeating this message of hope reaffirmed by the Second Vatican Council, which concluded forty years ago.

Men and women of today, humanity come of age yet often still so frail in mind and will, let the Child of Bethlehem take you by the hand! Do not fear; put your trust in him! The life-giving power of his light is an incentive for building a new world order based on just ethical and economic relationships. May his love guide every people on earth and strengthen their common consciousness of being a "family" called to foster relationships of trust and mutual support. A united humanity will be able to confront the many troubling problems of the present time: from the menace of terrorism to the humiliating poverty in which millions of human beings live, from the proliferation of weapons to the pandemics and the environmental destruction which threatens the future of our planet.

May the God who became man out of love for humanity strengthen all those in Africa who work for peace, integral development and the prevention of fratricidal conflicts, for the consolidation of the present, still fragile political transitions, and the protection of the most elementary rights of those experiencing tragic humanitarian crises, such as those in Darfur and in other regions of Central Africa. May he lead the peoples of Latin America to live in peace and harmony. May he grant courage to people of good will in the Holy Land, in Iraq, in Lebanon, where signs of hope, which are not lacking, need to be confirmed by actions inspired by fairness and wisdom; may he favor the process of dialogue on the Korean peninsula and elsewhere in the countries of Asia, so that, by the settlement of dangerous disputes, consistent and peaceful conclusions can be reached in a spirit of friendship, conclusions which their peoples expectantly await.

At Christmas we contemplate God made man, divine glory hidden beneath the poverty of a Child wrapped in swaddling clothes and laid in a manger; the Creator of the Universe reduced to the helplessness of an infant. Once we accept this paradox, we discover the Truth that sets us free and the Love that transforms our lives. On Bethlehem Night, the Redeemer becomes one of us, our companion along the precarious paths of history. Let us take the hand which he stretches out to us: it is a hand which seeks to take nothing from us, but only to give.

With the shepherds let us enter the stable of Bethlehem beneath the loving gaze of Mary, the silent witness of his miraculous birth. May she help us to experience the happiness of Christmas, may she teach us how to treasure in our hearts the mystery of God who for our sake became man; and may she help us to bear witness in our world to his truth, his love, and his peace.

Since I am unable to be present in person at the new and important meeting for the safeguard of creation, which you have organized with the Sixth Symposium on *"Religion, Science and the Environment,"* dedicated to the Amazon River, I entrust the task of bringing you my cordial greeting to Cardinal Roger Etchegaray.

I am grateful to you, Your Holiness, for having arranged that the preparation of the symposium take place in close collaboration with the Catholic Bishops' Conference of Brazil.

In fact, Cardinal Geraldo Majella Agnelo, Archbishop of São Salvador da Bahia, will be taking part and will not fail to express my gratitude to you for your support of the work of the Brazilian Episcopate in Amazonia and its action on behalf of the environment, whose deterioration has profound and serious repercussions on the population.

The joint effort to create awareness on the part of Christians of every denomination, in order to show "the intrinsic connection between development, human need and the stewardship of creation" (*Directory for the Application of the Principles and Norms of Ecumenism,* 1993, n. 215), is truly proving more important than ever.

In this context, I remember Pope John Paul II of venerable memory supporting the Fourth Symposium on the Adriatic Sea, and I also remember the Common Declaration that he signed with you, Venerable Brother.

The duty to emphasize an appropriate catechesis concerning creation, in order to recall the meaning and religious significance of protecting it, is closely connected with our duty as pastors and can have an important impact on the perception of the value of

---

4 Pope Benedict XVI, Letter to Bartholomew I, Ecumenical Patriarch on the Occasion of the Sixth Symposium on "Religion, Science, and the Environment" Focusing on the Amazon River, July 6, 2006.

life itself as well as on the satisfactory solution of the consequent inevitable social problems.

I warmly hope, Your Holiness, that the Sixth Symposium dedicated to the Amazon River will once again attract the attention of peoples and governments to the problems, needs, and emergencies of a region so harshly tried and whose ecological balance is so threatened: in their majestic beauty, its rivers and forests speak to us of God and of his grandiose work for humanity.

This immense region, where waters are an incomparable source of harmony and riches, is presented as an open book whose pages reveal the mystery of life.

How is it possible not to feel, both as individuals and as communities, urged to acquire a responsible awareness that is expressed in consistent decisions to protect such an ecologically rich environment?

With this symposium, Your Holiness, you have wished to express — over and above any other consideration, and there would be many of them — the Christian support for the peoples in the Amazon regions, a support, in short, that stems from contemplation of the eternal Word of God, the Author, Model, and End of all things.

As I express to you, Your Holiness, my deep appreciation of the intentions that inspire you, I would like to assure you of my support for the values inherent in the symposium. I see our common commitment as an example of that collaboration which Orthodox and Catholics must constantly seek, to respond to the call for a common witness.

This implies that all Christians seriously cultivate the mental openness that is dictated by love and rooted in faith. Thus they will be able together to offer to the world a credible witness of their sense of responsibility for the safeguard of creation.

At the Sixth Symposium dedicated to the Amazon River, prominent figures and experts will be taking part who belong to the great monotheistic religions. Their presence is important.

There are practical objectives that are a matter of survival for man and can, and must, bring together all people of good will.

Reciprocal respect also passes through projects such as this event, because the topics that will be addressed are of common interest to all.

Common points must be found on which converge the commitments of each one to safeguard the *habitat* that the Creator has made available to the human being, in whom he has impressed his own image.

Your Holiness, I ask you to convey my most cordial good wishes to all who are taking part in the symposium and to assure them of my prayers that it will constitute an important step forward in the effort, so widely shared, to safeguard this world that God created with wisdom and love (cf. Ps 104[103]).

I exchange a fraternal embrace with you, Your Holiness, in the Name of the One Lord.

INVESTING IN AGRICULTURE[5]

The annual celebration of World Food Day, sponsored by the Food and Agriculture Organization of the United Nations (FAO), is an opportunity to review the numerous activities of this organization, specifically with regard to its twofold aim: to provide adequate nutrition for our brothers and sisters throughout the world, and to consider the obstacles to this work caused by difficult situations and attitudes contrary to solidarity.

This year's chosen theme — *Investing in agriculture for food security* — focuses our attention on the agricultural sector and invites us to reflect on the various factors that hinder the fight against hunger, many of them man-made. Not enough attention is given to the needs of agriculture, and this both upsets the natural order of creation and compromises respect for human dignity.

In Christian tradition, agricultural labor takes on a deeper meaning, both because of the effort and hardship that it involves and also because it offers a privileged experience of God's presence and his love for his creatures. Christ himself uses agricultural images to speak of the Kingdom, thereby showing a great respect for this form of labor.

Today, we think especially of those who have had to abandon their farmlands because of conflicts, natural disasters and because of society's neglect of the agricultural sector. The "promotion of justice through efforts to bring about openness of mind and will to the demands of the common good is something which concerns the Church deeply" (Encyclical Letter *Deus Caritas Est*, 28).

---

5 Pope Benedict XVI, Message to the Director General of the Food and Agriculture Organization for the Celebration of World Food Day, October 16, 2006.

It is now ten years since my venerable predecessor, Pope John Paul II, inaugurated the *World Food Summit*. This gives us an opportunity to look back and take stock of the inadequate attention given to the agricultural sector and the effects this has on rural communities. Solidarity is the key to identifying and eliminating the causes of poverty and underdevelopment.

Very often, international action to combat hunger ignores the *human factor*, and priority is given instead to technical and socioeconomic aspects. Local communities need to be involved in choices and decisions concerning land use, since farmland is being diverted increasingly to other purposes, often with damaging effects on the environment and the long-term viability of the land. If the human person is treated as the protagonist, it becomes clear that short-term economic gains must be placed within the context of better long-term planning for food security, with regard to both quantity and quality.

The order of creation demands that priority be given to those human activities that do not cause irreversible damage to nature, but which instead are woven into the social, cultural, and religious fabric of the different communities. In this way, a sober balance is achieved between consumption and the sustainability of resources.

The *rural family* needs to regain its rightful place at the heart of the social order. The moral principles and values which govern it belong to the heritage of humanity, and must take priority over legislation. They are concerned with individual conduct, relations between husband and wife and between generations, and the sense of family solidarity. Investment in the agricultural sector has to allow the family to assume its proper place and function, avoiding the damaging consequences of hedonism and materialism that can place marriage and family life at risk.

Education and formation programs in rural areas need to be broadly based, adequately resourced, and aimed at all age groups. Special attention should be given to the most vulnerable, especially women and the young. It is important to hand on to future generations not merely the technical aspects of production, nutrition, and protection of natural resources, but the values of the rural world.

In faithfully carrying out its mandate, the FAO makes a vital investment in agriculture, not only through adequate technical and specialized support, but also by broadening the dialogue that takes place among the national and international agencies involved in rural development. Individual initiatives should be incorporated within larger strategies aimed at combating poverty and hunger. This can be of decisive importance if the nations and communities involved are to implement consistent programs and work toward a common goal.

Today more than ever, in the face of recurring crises and the pursuit of narrow self-interest, there has to be cooperation and solidarity between states, each of which should be attentive to the needs of its weakest citizens, who are the first to suffer from poverty. Without this solidarity, there is a risk of limiting or even impeding the work of international organizations that set out to fight hunger and malnutrition. In this way, they build up effectively the spirit of justice, harmony and peace among peoples: "*opus iustitiae pax*" (cf. Is 32:17).

With these thoughts, Director General, I wish to invoke the Lord's blessing upon FAO, its member states, and upon all those who work so hard to support the agricultural sector and to promote rural development.

5. Our concern extends to those parts of today's world where Christians live and to the difficulties they have to face, particularly poverty, wars, and terrorism, but equally to various forms of exploitation of the poor, of migrants, women, and children. We are called to work together to promote respect for the rights of every human being, created in the image and likeness of God, and to foster economic, social, and cultural development. Our theological and ethical traditions can offer a solid basis for a united approach in preaching and action. Above all, we wish to affirm that killing innocent people in God's name is an offence against him and against human dignity. We must all commit ourselves to the renewed service of humanity and the defense of human life, every human life.

We take profoundly to heart the cause of peace in the Middle East, where Our Lord lived, suffered, died, and rose again, and where a great multitude of our Christian brethren have lived for centuries. We fervently hope that peace will be re-established in that region, that respectful coexistence will be strengthened between the different peoples that live there, between the Churches and between the different religions found there. To this end, we encourage the establishment of closer relationships between Christians, and of an authentic and honest interreligious dialogue, with a view to combating every form of violence and discrimination.

6. At present, in the face of the great threats to the natural environment, we want to express our concern at the negative consequences for humanity and for the whole of creation which can result from economic and technological progress that does not know its limits. As religious leaders, we consider it one of

---

6 Pope Benedict XVI and Ecumenical Patriarch Bartholomew I, Common Declaration, Apostolic Journey to Turkey, November 30, 2006.

our duties to encourage and to support all efforts made to protect God's creation, and to bequeath to future generations a world in which they will be able to live.

7. Finally, our thoughts turn toward all of you, the faithful of our Churches throughout the world, Bishops, priests, deacons, men and women religious, laymen and women engaged in ecclesial service, and all the baptized. In Christ we greet other Christians, assuring them of our prayers and our openness to dialogue and cooperation. In the words of the Apostle of the Gentiles, we greet all of you: "Grace to you and peace from God our Father and the Lord Jesus Christ" (2 Cor 1:2).

From the Phanar, November 30, 2006

8. In his Encyclical Letter *Centesimus Annus*, Pope John Paul II wrote: "Not only has God given the earth to man, who must use it with respect for the original good purpose for which it was given to him, but man too is God's gift to man. He must therefore respect the natural and moral structure with which he has been endowed" (No. 38). By responding to this charge, entrusted to them by the Creator, men and women can join in bringing about a world of peace. Alongside the ecology of nature, there exists what can be called a "human" ecology, which in turn demands a "social" ecology. All this means that humanity, if it truly desires peace, must be increasingly conscious of the links between natural ecology, or respect for nature, and human ecology. Experience shows that *disregard for the environment always harms human coexistence*, and vice versa. It becomes more and more evident that there is an inseparable link between peace with creation and peace among men. Both of these presuppose peace with God. The poem-prayer of Saint Francis, known as "The Canticle of Brother Sun," is a wonderful and ever timely example of this multifaceted ecology of peace.

9. The close connection between these two ecologies can be understood from the increasingly serious problem of *energy supplies*. In recent years, new nations have entered enthusiastically into industrial production, thereby increasing their energy needs. This has led to an unprecedented race for available resources. Meanwhile, some parts of the planet remain backward and development is effectively blocked, partly because of the rise in energy prices. What will happen to those peoples? What kind of development or nondevelopment will be imposed on them

---

7 Pope Benedict XVI, Message for the Celebration of the World Day of Peace, January 1, 2007.

by the scarcity of energy supplies? What injustices and conflicts will be provoked by the race for energy sources? And what will be the reaction of those who are excluded from this race? These are questions that show how respect for nature is closely linked to the need to establish, between individuals and between nations, relationships that are attentive to the dignity of the person and capable of satisfying his or her authentic needs.

The destruction of the environment, its improper or selfish use, and the violent hoarding of the earth's resources cause grievances, conflicts, and wars, precisely because they are the consequences of an inhumane concept of development. Indeed, if development were limited to the technical-economic aspect, obscuring the moral-religious dimension, it would not be an integral human development, but a one-sided distortion which would end up by unleashing man's destructive capacities.

REDUCTIVE VISIONS OF MAN

10. Thus there is an urgent need, even within the framework of current international difficulties and tensions, for a commitment to *a human ecology that can favor the growth of the "tree of peace."* For this to happen, we must be guided by a vision of the person untainted by ideological and cultural prejudices or by political and economic interests which can instill hatred and violence. It is understandable that visions of man will vary from culture to culture. Yet what cannot be admitted is the cultivation of *anthropological conceptions* that contain the seeds of hostility and violence. Equally unacceptable are *conceptions of God* that would encourage intolerance and recourse to violence against others. This is a point which must be clearly reaffirmed: War *in God's name* is never acceptable! When a certain notion of God is at the

origin of criminal acts, it is a sign that that notion has already become an ideology.

11. Today, however, peace is not only threatened by the conflict between reductive visions of man, in other words, between ideologies. It is also threatened by *indifference as to what constitutes man's true nature*. Many of our contemporaries actually deny the existence of a specific human nature and thus open the door to the most extravagant interpretations of what essentially constitutes a human being. Here too clarity is necessary: a "weak" vision of the person, which would leave room for every conception, even the most bizarre, only apparently favors peace. In reality, it hinders authentic dialogue and opens the way to authoritarian impositions, ultimately leaving the person defenseless and, as a result, easy prey to oppression and violence.

THE CHURCH'S SOCIAL TEACHING

91. The mystery of the Eucharist inspires and impels us to work courageously within our world to bring about that renewal of relationships which has its inexhaustible source in God's gift. The prayer which we repeat at every Mass, "Give us this day our daily bread," obliges us to do everything possible, in cooperation with international, state, and private institutions, to end or at least reduce the scandal of hunger and malnutrition afflicting so many millions of people in our world, especially in developing countries. In a particular way, the Christian laity, formed at the school of the Eucharist, are called to assume their specific political and social responsibilities. To do so, they need to be adequately prepared through practical education in charity and justice. To this end, the synod considered it necessary for dioceses and Christian communities to teach and promote the Church's social doctrine. (248) In this precious legacy handed down from the earliest ecclesial tradition, we find elements of great wisdom that guide Christians in their involvement in today's burning social issues. This teaching, the fruit of the Church's whole history, is distinguished by realism and moderation; it can help to avoid misguided compromises or false utopias.

THE SANCTIFICATION OF THE WORLD AND THE PROTECTION OF CREATION

92. Finally, to develop a profound eucharistic spirituality that is also capable of significantly affecting the fabric of society, the Christian people, in giving thanks to God through the Eucharist, should be conscious that they do so in the name of all creation,

---

8 Pope Benedict XVI, Apostolic Exhortation *Sacramentum Caritatis,* February 22, 2007.

aspiring to the sanctification of the world and working intensely to that end. (249) The Eucharist itself powerfully illuminates human history and the whole cosmos. In this sacramental perspective we learn, day by day, that every ecclesial event is a kind of sign by which God makes himself known and challenges us. The eucharistic form of life can thus help foster a real change in the way we approach history and the world. The liturgy itself teaches us this, when, during the presentation of the gifts, the priest raises to God a prayer of blessing and petition over the bread and wine, "fruit of the earth," "fruit of the vine," and "work of human hands." With these words, the rite not only includes in our offering to God all human efforts and activity, but also leads us to see the world as God's creation, which brings forth everything we need for our sustenance.

The world is not something indifferent, raw material to be utilized simply as we see fit. Rather, it is part of God's good plan, in which all of us are called to be sons and daughters in the one Son of God, Jesus Christ (cf. Eph 1:4-12). The justified concern about threats to the environment present in so many parts of the world is reinforced by Christian hope, which commits us to working responsibly for the protection of creation. (250) The relationship between the Eucharist and the cosmos helps us to see the unity of God's plan and to grasp the profound relationship between creation and the "new creation" inaugurated in the resurrection of Christ, the new Adam. Even now we take part in that new creation by virtue of our baptism (cf. Col 2:12ff.). Our Christian life, nourished by the Eucharist, gives us a glimpse of that new world — new heavens and a new earth — where the new Jerusalem comes down from heaven, from God, "prepared as a bride adorned for her husband" (Rv 21:2).

On the occasion of today's celebration of World Water Day, His Holiness Benedict XVI charges me to convey to you, Mr. Director General, and to all the participants at this meeting, respectful and cordial greetings and encouragement for your action in favor of those in the world who are suffering from a shortage of water.

In the context of the Decade 2005/2015, which the General Assembly of the United Nations has declared *"The International Decade of Action: Water for life,"* this year's theme: *Coping with water scarcity*, gives us an opportunity to think about the importance of water as a source of life whose availability is essential for the vital cycles of the earth and fundamental for a fully human existence.

We are all aware of the difficulty of achieving at a world level the goal fixed by the international community to halve the number of people who are without access to healthy water and basic hygiene services by 2015 through the development, among other things, of integrated management plans and an efficient use of water resources.

However, we are likewise all convinced of the importance of not falling short of these goals, given the centrality of water in any process destined to foster the promotion of an integral human development.

Furthermore, appropriate investments in the sector of water and hygiene services represent a significant mechanism for accelerating economic growth and sustainable development, for improving human health and hygiene, for uprooting poverty, and for combating the degradation of the environment.

---

9 Message of Pope Benedict XVI, Signed by Cardinal Tarcisio Bertone to the Director of FAO on the Occasion of the Celebration of World Water Day, March 22, 2007.

Water, a common good of the human family, constitutes an essential element for life; the management of this precious resource must enable all to have access to it, especially those who live in conditions of poverty, and must guarantee the liveability of the planet for both the present and future generations.

Access to water is in fact one of the inalienable rights of every human being, because it is a prerequisite for the realization of the majority of the other human rights, such as the rights to life, to food, and to health.

For this reason, water "cannot be treated as just another commodity among many, and it must be used rationally and in solidarity with others.... The right to water ... finds its basis in human dignity and not in any kind of merely quantitative assessment that considers water as a merely economic good. Without water, life is threatened. Therefore, the right to safe drinking water is a universal and inalienable right" (*Compendium of the Social Doctrine of the Church,* No. 485).

World Water Day is a precious opportunity to encourage the international community to identify effective ways to permit this basic human right to be promoted, protected and enjoyed. In this regard, the sustainable management of water becomes a social, economic, environmental, and ethical challenge that involves not only institutions but the whole of society.

It should be faced in accordance with the principle of subsidiarity, that is, through the adoption of a participatory approach that involves both the private sector and above all the local communities; the principle of solidarity, a fundamental pillar of international cooperation, which requires a preferential attention to the poor; the principle of responsibility to the present generation and those to come, from which derives the consequent need to re-examine the models of consumption and production, often unsustainable with regard to the use of water resources.

It is in addition a responsibility that must be shared and that becomes a moral and political imperative in a world that has levels of know-how and technologies that are capable of putting an end to situations of water scarcity and to their dramatic consequences that affect in particular the regions with a lower income, in which access to water can often spark real conflicts, whereas it can become a motive for interregional cooperation wherever people appreciate a farsighted approach founded on hydrological interdependence that binds those who use the water resource in neighboring countries in a joint agreement.

These are aspects, Mr. Director General, that not only demand the responsibility of government leaders and politicians, but that challenge every individual. We are all called to renew our lifestyles with an educational effort that can reassign to this common good of humanity the value and respect that it ought to have in our society.

Moreover, an educational effort of this kind could draw from many sacred texts of the traditional religions, such as the Bible, where water is symbolically a source and a sign of life, and its presence is often associated with joy and fertility, assuming in addition a role of purification, renewal, and rebirth.

On this World Water Day, the Holy Father invokes the Lord's blessings on all those who are committed to reaching the goals concerning water that have been set by the international community. Mr. Director General, I am honored to convey to you this message from His Holiness and ask you to accept the expression of my highest esteem.

Cardinal Tarcisio Bertone
Secretary of State of His Holiness

Recalling the "Note" that Pope Benedict XV addressed to the belligerent countries in the First World War on August 1 ninety years ago, I dwelled on the theme of peace.

Now a new occasion invites me to reflect on another important subject connected with this theme. Precisely today, in fact, is the fiftieth anniversary of the establishment of the Charter of the IAEA, the *International Atomic Energy Agency,* instituted with the mandate to "accelerate and enlarge the contribution of atomic energy to peace, health and prosperity throughout the world" (art. 2).

The Holy See, fully approving the goals of this organization, is a member of it since its founding and continues to support its activity.

The epochal changes that have occurred in the last fifty years demonstrate how, in the difficult crossroads in which humanity finds itself, the commitment to encourage nonproliferation of nuclear arms, to promote a progressive and agreed upon nuclear disarmament, and to support the use of peaceful and safe nuclear technology for authentic development, respecting the environment and ever mindful of the most disadvantaged populations, is always more present and urgent.

I therefore hope that the efforts of those who work with determination to bring about these three objectives may be achieved, with the goal that "the resources which would be saved could then be employed in projects of development capable of benefiting all their people, especially the poor" (*Message for the World Day of Peace 2006*).

It is also good on this occasion to repeat how: "In place of ... the arms race, there must be substituted a common effort

---

10 Pope Benedict XVI, Angelus, July 29, 2007.

to mobilize resources toward objectives of moral, cultural and economic development, "redefining the priorities and hierarchies of values'" (*Catechism of the Catholic Church*, No. 2438).

Again we entrust to the intercession of Mary Most Holy our prayer for peace, in particular so that scientific knowledge and technology are always applied with a sense of responsibility and for the common good, in full respect for international rights.

Let us pray so that men live in peace and that they may be as brothers, sons of one Father: God.

I would simply like to [provide] catechesis on the life and writings of Saint Basil, a bishop ... in Asia Minor [present-day Turkey] in the fourth century A.D. The life and works of this great saint are full of ideas for reflection and teachings that are also relevant for us today.

First of all is the reference to *God's mystery,* which is still the most meaningful and vital reference for human beings. The Father is "the principal of all things and the cause of being of all that exists, the root of the living" (*Hom.* 15, 2 *de fide: PG* 31, 465c); above all, he is "the Father of Our Lord Jesus Christ" (*Anaphora Sancti Basilii*). Ascending to God through his creatures, we "become aware of his goodness and wisdom" (Basil, *Adversus Eunomium* 1, 14: *PG* 29, 544b).

The Son is the "image of the Father's goodness and seal in the same form" (cf. *Anaphora Sancti Basilii).* With his obedience and his Passion, the Incarnate Word carried out his mission as Redeemer of man (cf. Basil, *In Psalmum* 48, 8; *PG* 29, 452ab; cf. also *De Baptismo* 1, 2: *SC* 357, 158).

Lastly, he spoke fully of the Holy Spirit, to whom he dedicated a whole book. He reveals to us that the Spirit enlivens the Church, fills her with his gifts and sanctifies her.

The resplendent light of the divine mystery is reflected in man, the image of God, and exalts his dignity. Looking at Christ, one fully understands human dignity. Basil exclaims: "[Man], be mindful of your greatness, remembering the price paid for you: look at the price of your redemption and comprehend your dignity!" (*In Psalmum* 48, 8: *PG* 29, 452b).

Christians in particular, conforming their lives to the Gospel, recognize that all people are brothers and sisters; that life is a

---

11 Pope Benedict XVI, General Audience, August 1, 2007.

stewardship of the goods received from God, which is why each one is responsible for the other, and whoever is rich must be as it were an "executor of the orders of God the Benefactor" (*Hom. 6 de avaritia: PG* 32, 1181-1196). We must all help one another and cooperate as members of one body (*Ep* 203, 3).

And on this point, he used courageous, strong words in his homilies. Indeed, anyone who desires to love his neighbor as himself, in accordance with God's commandment, "must possess no more than his neighbor" (*Hom. in divites: PG* 31, 281b).

In times of famine and disaster, the holy bishop exhorted the faithful with passionate words "not to be more cruel than beasts ... by taking over what people possess in common or by grabbing what belongs to all" (*Hom. tempore famis: PG* 31, 325a).

Basil's profound thought stands out in this evocative sentence: "All the destitute look to our hands just as we look to those of God when we are in need."

Therefore, Gregory of Nazianzus' praise after Basil's death was well-deserved. He said: "Basil convinces us that since we are human beings, we must neither despise men nor offend Christ, the common Head of all, with our inhuman behavior toward people; rather, we ourselves must benefit by learning from the misfortunes of others and must lend God our compassion, for we are in need of mercy" (Gregory Nazianzus, *Orationes* 43, 63; *PG* 36, 580b).

These words are very timely. We see that Saint Basil is truly one of the Fathers of the Church's social doctrine.

It gives me great joy to greet all those taking part in the Seventh Symposium of the Religion, Science and the Environment movement, which this year turns its attention to the subject, "The Arctic: Mirror of Life." Your own dedication and personal commitment to the protection of the environment demonstrates the pressing need for science and religion to work together to safeguard the gifts of nature and to promote responsible stewardship. Through the presence of Cardinal [Theodore] McCarrick I wish to reaffirm my fervent solidarity with the aims of the project and to assure you of my hope for a deepening global recognition of the vital relationship between the ecology of the human person and the ecology of nature (cf. Message for the 2007 World Day of Peace, 8).

Preservation of the environment, promotion of sustainable development and particular attention to climate change are matters of grave concern for the entire human family. No nation or business sector can ignore the ethical implications present in all economic and social development. With increasing clarity scientific research demonstrates that the impact of human actions in any one place or region can have worldwide effects. The consequences of disregard for the environment cannot be limited to an immediate area or populus because they always harm human coexistence, and thus betray human dignity and violate the rights of citizens who desire to live in a safe environment (cf. *ibid.*, 8-9).

This year's symposium, dedicated again to the earth's water resources, takes you and various religious leaders, scientists, and other interested parties to the Ilulissat Icefjord on the west coast

---

12   Pope Benedict XVI, Letter to the Ecumenical Patriarch of Constantinople on the Occasion of the Seventh Symposium of the Religion, Science and the Environment Movement, September 1, 2007.

of Greenland. Gathered in the magnificent beauty of this unique glacial region and World Heritage site your hearts and minds turn readily to the wonders of God and in awe echo the words of the Psalmist praising the name of the Lord who is "majestic in all the earth." Immersed in contemplation of the "work of his fingers" (Ps 8), the perils of spiritual alienation from creation become plainly evident. The relationship between individuals or communities and the environment ultimately stems from their relationship with God. When "man turns his back on the Creator's plan, he provokes a disorder which has inevitable repercussions on the rest of the created order" (*Message for the 1990 World Day of Peace*, 5).

Your Holiness, the international and multidisciplinary nature of the symposium attests to the need to seek global solutions to the matters under consideration. I am encouraged by the growing recognition that the entire human community — children and adults, industry sectors, states and international bodies — must take seriously the responsibility that falls to each and every one of us. While it is true that industrializing countries are not morally free to repeat the past errors of others, by recklessly continuing to damage the environment (cf. *ibid.*, 10), it is also the case that highly industrialized countries must share "clean technologies" and ensure that their own markets do not sustain demand for goods whose very production contributes to the proliferation of pollution. Mutual interdependence between nations' economic and social activities demands international solidarity, cooperation, and ongoing educational efforts. It is these principles which the Religion, Science and the Environment movement courageously upholds.

With sentiments of deep appreciation, and mindful of our commitment to encourage and support all efforts made to protect God's works (cf. *Common Declaration,* November 30, 2006), I pray that the Almighty will abundantly bless this year's symposium. May he accompany you and all those gathered with you, so that all creation may give praise to God!

1. This year the United Nations' Food and Agriculture Organization (FAO), which you direct, invites the international community, remembering once again its foundation, to tackle one of the gravest challenges of our time: freeing millions of human beings from hunger, whose lives are in danger due to a lack of daily bread.

The theme chosen for this day, *"The right to food,"* fittingly opens the reflections that the international community is preparing to make on the occasion of the sixtieth anniversary of the Universal Declaration of Human Rights. This coincidence helps us to recall the importance that the right to food has for the realization of other rights, beginning above all with the fundamental right to life.

We must observe that the endeavors made until now have not significantly diminished the numbers of those suffering from hunger in the world, even though all know that food is a primary right. This is perhaps due to the fact that one tends to be solely and principally motivated by technical and economic considerations, forgetting the primary, ethical dimension of "feeding the hungry."

This priority concerns the sentiments of compassion and solidarity proper to the human being, which includes sharing with others not only material goods, but also the love which all need. In effect, we give too little if we offer only material things.

2. The available data show that the nonfulfillment of the right to food is not only due to natural causes, but also and above all to situations provoked by the conduct of men and women that lead to a general deterioration of social, economic, and human standards.

---

13 Pope Benedict XVI, Message to the General Director of the Food and Agriculture Organization of the United Nations, October 4, 2007.

Increasingly, there are always more people who, because of poverty and bloody conflicts, feel obligated to leave their own home and loved ones in order to search for support outside their own country. In spite of international pledges, many of these people are refused.

Among the mature members of the Community of Nations, however, a strong awareness is needed that considers food as a universal right of all human beings, without distinction or discrimination.

3. The objective of eradicating hunger, and at the same time of being able to provide healthy and sufficient food, also demands specific methods and actions that mean a wise use of resources that respect Creation's patrimony.

The result of working in this direction will benefit not only science, research and technology, but also take into account the cycles and rhythm of nature known to the inhabitants of rural areas, thus protecting the traditional customs of the indigenous communities, leaving aside egotistical and exclusively economic motivations.

The right to food, with all that this implies, has an immediate repercussion on both the individual and communal dimensions, which bring together entire peoples and human groups. I am thinking in a special way of the situation of children — the main victims of this tragedy — who at times are obstacles to their physical and psychological development and in many instances are forced to work or are enlisted in armed groups in exchange for a little food.

In such cases, I place my hope in the initiatives that have been proposed on many levels in favor of school food programs and which permit the entire community, whose survival is threatened by hunger, to look with great hope to the future.

A common and concrete commitment is therefore urgently needed in which all members of society, both in the individual as well as the international spheres, feel duty-bound to work together in order to actualize the right to food, for failure to do so constitutes a clear violation of human dignity and of the rights which derive from it.

4. Knowledge of the problems of the agricultural world and of a lack of food, demonstrated by a capacity to propose plans and programs to find solutions, is a fundamental merit of the FAO and testifies to the acute sensibility for the aspirations of those conditions put forward for a more human life.

At this time when there are so many similar problems, it would also be well to find new initiatives that can contribute to alleviating the drama of hunger, and I encourage you to continue to work so that food may be guaranteed that responds to actual needs, and in such a way, that every person, created in the image of God, may grow conformed to his true human dimension.

The Catholic Church feels close to you in this endeavor and, throughout your diverse institutions, desires to continue to collaborate in order to sustain the aspirations and hopes of those persons and those peoples for which the work of the FAO is directed.

These are, Mr. Director General, some reflections that I wish to bring to the attention of those who, with different responsibilities, work to offer the human family a future free of the drama of hunger, and at the same time I invoke upon you and your work the constant blessing of the Most High.

Today, November 11, the Church remembers Saint Martin, Bishop of Tours, one of the most celebrated and venerated saints of Europe. Born of pagan parents in Pannonia, in what is today Hungary, he was directed by his father to a military career around the year 316. Still an adolescent, Martin came into contact with Christianity and, overcoming many difficulties, he enrolled as a catechumen in order to prepare for baptism. He would receive the sacrament in his twenties, but he would still stay for a long time in the army, where he would give testimony of his new lifestyle: respectful and inclusive of all, he treated his attendant as a brother and avoided vulgar entertainment. Leaving military service, he went to Poitiers in France near the holy Bishop Hilary. He was ordained a deacon and priest by him, chose the monastic life, and with some disciples established the oldest monastery known in Europe at Ligugé. About ten years later, the Christians of Tours, who were without a pastor, acclaimed him their bishop. From that time, Martin dedicated himself with ardent zeal to the evangelization of the countryside and the formation of the clergy. While many miracles are attributed to him, St. Martin is known most of all for an act of fraternal charity. While still a young soldier, he met a poor man on the street numb and trembling from the cold. He then took his own cloak and, cutting it in two with his sword, gave half to that man. Jesus appeared to him that night in a dream smiling, dressed in the same cloak.

Dear brothers and sisters, Saint Martin's charitable gesture flows from the same logic that drove Jesus to multiply the loaves for the hungry crowd, but most of all to leave himself to humanity as food in the Eucharist, supreme Sign of God's love, *Sacramentum caritatis*. It is the logic of sharing which he used to

---

14   Pope Benedict XVI, Angelus, November 11, 2007.

authentically explain love of neighbor. May Saint Martin help us to understand that only by means of a common commitment to sharing is it possible to respond to the great challenge of our times: to build a world of peace and justice where each person can live with dignity. This can be achieved if a world model of authentic solidarity prevails which assures to all inhabitants of the planet food, water, necessary medical treatment, and also work and energy resources, as well as cultural benefits, scientific, and technological knowledge.

Let us turn now to the Virgin Mary so that all Christians may be like Saint Martin, generous witnesses of the Gospel of love and tireless builders of jointly responsible sharing.

16. How could the idea have developed that Jesus' message is narrowly individualistic and aimed only at each person singly? How did we arrive at this interpretation of the "salvation of the soul" as a flight from responsibility for the whole, and how did we come to conceive the Christian project as a selfish search for salvation which rejects the idea of serving others? In order to find an answer to this we must take a look at the foundations of the modern age. These appear with particular clarity in the thought of Francis Bacon. That a new era emerged — through the discovery of America and the new technical achievements that had made this development possible — is undeniable. But what is the basis of this new era? It is the new correlation of experiment and method that enables man to arrive at an interpretation of nature in conformity with its laws and thus finally to achieve "the triumph of art over nature" (*victoria cursus artis super naturam*) (*Novum Organum* I, 117). The novelty — according to Bacon's vision — lies in a new correlation between science and praxis. This is also given a theological application: the new correlation between science and praxis would mean that the dominion over creation — given to man by God and lost through original sin — would be re-established (cf. *ibid.* I, 129).

17. Anyone who reads and reflects on these statements attentively will recognize that a disturbing step has been taken: up to that time, the recovery of what man had lost through the expulsion from Paradise was expected from faith in Jesus Christ: herein lay "redemption." Now, this "redemption," the restoration of the lost "Paradise," is no longer expected from faith, but from the newly discovered link between science and praxis. It is not that faith is simply denied; rather it is displaced onto another

15 Pope Benedict XVI, Encyclical Letter *Spe Salvi* (In Hope We Are Saved), November 30, 2007.

level — that of purely private and otherworldly affairs — and at the same time it becomes somehow irrelevant for the world. This programmatic vision has determined the trajectory of modern times, and it also shapes the present-day crisis of faith which is essentially a crisis of Christian hope. Thus hope too, in Bacon, acquires a new form. Now it is called: *faith in progress*. For Bacon, it is clear that the recent spate of discoveries and inventions is just the beginning; through the interplay of science and praxis, totally new discoveries will follow, a totally new world will emerge, the kingdom of man (cf. *New Atlantis*). He even put forward a vision of foreseeable inventions — including the airplane and the submarine. As the ideology of progress developed further, joy at visible advances in human potential remained a continuing confirmation of *faith in progress* as such.

18. At the same time, two categories become increasingly central to the idea of progress: reason and freedom. Progress is primarily associated with the growing dominion of reason, and this reason is obviously considered to be a force of good and a force for good. Progress is the overcoming of all forms of dependency — it is progress toward perfect freedom. Likewise freedom is seen purely as a promise, in which man becomes more and more fully himself. In both concepts — freedom and reason — there is a political aspect. The kingdom of reason, in fact, is expected as the new condition of the human race once it has attained total freedom. The political conditions of such a kingdom of reason and freedom, however, appear at first sight somewhat ill defined. Reason and freedom seem to guarantee by themselves, by virtue of their intrinsic goodness, a new and perfect human community. The two key concepts of "reason" and "freedom," however, were tacitly interpreted as being in conflict with the shackles of faith and of the Church, as well as those of

the political structures of the period. Both concepts therefore contain a revolutionary potential of enormous explosive force....

22. Again, we find ourselves facing the question: what may we hope? A self-critique of modernity is needed in dialogue with Christianity and its concept of hope. In this dialogue Christians too, in the context of their knowledge and experience, must learn anew in what their hope truly consists, what they have to offer to the world, and what they cannot offer. Flowing into this self-critique of the modern age there also has to be a self-critique of modern Christianity, which must constantly renew its self-understanding setting out from its roots. On this subject, all we can attempt here are a few brief observations.

First we must ask ourselves: what does "progress" really mean; what does it promise and what does it not promise? In the nineteenth century, faith in progress was already subject to critique. In the twentieth century, Theodor W. Adorno formulated the problem of faith in progress quite drastically: he said that progress, seen accurately, is progress from the sling to the atom bomb. Now this is certainly an aspect of progress that must not be concealed. To put it another way: the ambiguity of progress becomes evident. Without doubt, it offers new possibilities for good, but it also opens up appalling possibilities for evil — possibilities that formerly did not exist. We have all witnessed the way in which progress, in the wrong hands, can become, and has indeed become, a terrifying progress in evil. If technical progress is not matched by corresponding progress in man's ethical formation, in man's inner growth (cf. Eph 3:16; 2 Cor 4:16), then it is not progress at all, but a threat for man and for the world.

23. As far as the two great themes of "reason" and "freedom" are concerned, here we can only touch upon the issues connected with them. Yes indeed, reason is God's great gift to man, and the

victory of reason over unreason is also a goal of the Christian life. But when does reason truly triumph? When it is detached from God? When it has become blind to God? Is the reason behind action and capacity for action the whole of reason? If progress, in order to be progress, needs moral growth on the part of humanity, then the reason behind action and capacity for action is likewise urgently in need of integration through reason's openness to the saving forces of faith, to the differentiation between good and evil. Only thus does reason become truly human. It becomes human only if it is capable of directing the will along the right path, and it is capable of this only if it looks beyond itself. Otherwise, man's situation, in view of the imbalance between his material capacity and the lack of judgment in his heart, becomes a threat for him and for creation.

Thus where freedom is concerned, we must remember that human freedom always requires a convergence of various freedoms. Yet this convergence cannot succeed unless it is determined by a common intrinsic criterion of measurement, which is the foundation and goal of our freedom. Let us put it very simply: man needs God, otherwise he remains without hope. Given the developments of the modern age, the quotation from Saint Paul with which I began (Eph 2:12) proves to be thoroughly realistic and plainly true. There is no doubt, therefore, that a "kingdom of God" accomplished without God — a kingdom therefore of man alone — inevitably ends up as the "perverse end" of all things as described by Kant: we have seen it, and we see it over and over again. Yet neither is there any doubt that God truly enters into human affairs only when, rather than being present merely in our thinking, he himself comes toward us and speaks to us. Reason therefore needs faith if it is to be completely itself: reason and faith need one another in order to fulfill their true nature and their mission....

35. All serious and upright human conduct is hope in action. This is so, first of all, in the sense that we thereby strive to realize our lesser and greater hopes, to complete this or that task which is important for our onward journey, or we work toward a brighter and more humane world so as to open doors into the future. Yet our daily efforts in pursuing our own lives and in working for the world's future either tire us or turn into fanaticism, unless we are enlightened by the radiance of the great hope that cannot be destroyed even by small-scale failures or by a breakdown in matters of historic importance. If we cannot hope for more than is effectively attainable at any given time, or more than is promised by political or economic authorities, our lives will soon be without hope. It is important to know that I can always continue to hope, even if in my own life, or the historical period in which I am living, there seems to be nothing left to hope for. Only the great certitude of hope that my own life and history in general, despite all failures, are held firm by the indestructible power of Love, and that this gives them their meaning and importance, only this kind of hope can then give the courage to act and to persevere.

Certainly we cannot "build" the kingdom of God by our own efforts — what we build will always be the kingdom of man with all the limitations proper to our human nature. The kingdom of God is a gift, and precisely because of this, it is great and beautiful, and constitutes the response to our hope. And we cannot — to use the classical expression — "merit" heaven through our works. Heaven is always more than we could merit, just as being loved is never something "merited," but always a gift. However, even when we are fully aware that heaven far exceeds what we can merit, it will always be true that our behavior is not indifferent before God and therefore is not indifferent for the unfolding of history. We can open ourselves and the world and allow God to enter: we can open ourselves to truth, to love, to what is good. This is what the saints did, those who, as "God's fellow workers," contributed to the world's salvation (cf. 1 Cor 3:9; 1 Thes 3:2).

We can free our life and the world from the poisons and contaminations that could destroy the present and the future. We can uncover the sources of creation and keep them unsullied, and in this way we can make a right use of creation, which comes to us as a gift, according to its intrinsic requirements and ultimate purpose. This makes sense even if outwardly we achieve nothing or seem powerless in the face of overwhelming hostile forces. So on the one hand, our actions engender hope for us and for others; but at the same time, it is the great hope based upon God's promises that gives us courage and directs our action in good times and bad.

I remember most vividly the day I spent at the *Fazenda da Esperança,* where people enslaved by drugs rediscover freedom and hope. On my arrival there, the first thing that happened was that I perceived the healing power of God's creation in a new way. Green mountains encircle the broad valley; they direct the gaze upward and at the same time give a sense of protection. From the tabernacle of the little church of the Carmelites flows a stream of clear water which calls to mind Ezekiel's prophecy about the water flowing from the Temple which disintoxicates the salty earth, making possible the growth of trees that bring life. We must defend creation not only with a view to its usefulness for us but for its own sake — as a message from the Creator, a gift of beauty which is a promise and hope. Yes, man needs transcendence. God alone suffices, Teresa of Avila said.

If God is absent, man must seek by himself to go beyond the world's boundaries, to open before him the boundless space for which he was created. Drugs then become, as it were, a need for him. Yet he very soon discovers that they are an unending illusion — one might say, a trick the devil plays on man. There, at the *Fazenda da Esperança,* the world's boundaries are truly transcended, the gaze is opened to God, to the fullness of our life, and so healing is brought about. I address my sincere gratitude to all those who work there and my cordial good wishes and blessings to all who seek healing there.

I would then like to recall the meeting with the Brazilian bishops in the Cathedral of Sao Paulo (May 11, 2007). The solemn music that accompanied us lives on, unforgettable. What made it particularly beautiful was the fact that it was performed by a choir and orchestra composed of poor youth from that city.

---

16 Pope Benedict XVI, Address, December 21, 2007.

Those people thus offered us the experience of beauty, one of those gifts through which it is possible to go beyond the limitations of the everyday nature of the world and perceive loftier realities that assure us of God's beauty. Then the experience of "effective and affective collegiality," of fraternal communion in our common ministry, made us feel the joy of catholicity. Beyond all the geographical and cultural boundaries we are brothers and sisters, together with the Risen Christ who has called us to his service.

In the silence of that night in Bethlehem, Jesus was born and lovingly welcomed. And now, on this Christmas Day, when the joyful news of his saving birth continues to resound, who is ready to open the doors of his heart to the holy child? Men and women of this modern age, Christ comes also to us bringing his light, he comes also to us granting peace! But who is watching, in the night of doubt and uncertainty, with a vigilant, praying heart? Who is waiting for the dawn of the new day, keeping alight the flame of faith? Who has time to listen to his word and to become enfolded and entranced by his love? Yes! His message of peace is for everyone; he comes to offer himself to all people as sure hope for salvation.

Finally, may the light of Christ, which comes to enlighten every human being, shine forth and bring consolation to those who live in the darkness of poverty, injustice and war; to those who are still denied their legitimate aspirations for a more secure existence, for health, education, stable employment, for fuller participation in civil and political responsibilities, free from oppression and protected from conditions that offend against human dignity. It is the most vulnerable members of society — women, children, the elderly — who are so often the victims of brutal armed conflicts, terrorism, and violence of every kind, which inflict such terrible sufferings on entire populations. At the same time, ethnic, religious and political tensions, instability, rivalry, disagreements, and all forms of injustice and discrimination are destroying the internal fabric of many countries and embittering international relations.

Throughout the world the number of migrants, refugees, and evacuees is also increasing because of frequent natural disasters, often caused by alarming environmental upheavals.

---

17 Pope Benedict XVI, *Urbi et Orbi* Message, Christmas 2007.

A Home for the Family[18]

1. At the beginning of a New Year, I wish to send my fervent good wishes for peace, together with a heartfelt message of hope to men and women throughout the world. I do so by offering for our common reflection the theme which I have placed at the beginning of this message. It is one which I consider particularly important: *the human family, a community of peace*. The first form of communion between persons is that born of the love of a man and a woman who decide to enter a stable union in order to build together *a new family*. But the peoples of the earth, too, are called to build relationships of solidarity and cooperation among themselves, as befits members of the one *human family*: "All peoples" — as the Second Vatican Council declared — "are one community and have one origin, because God caused the whole human race to dwell on the face of the earth (cf. Acts 17:26); they also have one final end, God" (Declaration *Nostra Aetate*, No. 1)....

THE FAMILY, THE HUMAN COMMUNITY AND THE ENVIRONMENT

7. The family needs a home, a fit environment in which to develop its proper relationships. *For the human family, this home is the earth*, the environment that God the Creator has given us to inhabit with creativity and responsibility. We need to care for the environment: it has been entrusted to men and women to be protected and cultivated with responsible freedom, with the good of all as a constant guiding criterion. Human beings, obviously, are of supreme worth vis-à-vis creation as a whole. Respecting the environment does not mean considering material or animal nature more important than man. Rather, it means not

---

18 Pope Benedict XVI, Message for the Celebration of the World Day of Peace, January 1, 2008.

selfishly considering nature to be at the complete disposal of our own interests, for future generations also have the right to reap its benefits and to exhibit toward nature the same responsible freedom that we claim for ourselves.

Nor must we overlook the poor, who are excluded in many cases from the goods of creation destined for all. Humanity today is rightly concerned about the ecological balance of tomorrow. It is important for assessments in this regard to be carried out prudently, in dialogue with experts and people of wisdom, uninhibited by ideological pressure to draw hasty conclusions, and above all with the aim of reaching agreement on a model of sustainable development capable of ensuring the well-being of all while respecting environmental balances.

If the protection of the environment involves costs, they should be justly distributed, taking due account of the different levels of development of various countries and the need for solidarity with future generations. Prudence does not mean failing to accept responsibilities and postponing decisions; it means being committed to making joint decisions after pondering responsibly the road to be taken, decisions aimed at strengthening that covenant between human beings and the environment, which should mirror the creative love of God, from whom we come and toward whom we are journeying.

8. In this regard, it is essential to "sense" that the earth is "our common home" and, in our stewardship and service to all, to choose the path of dialogue rather than the path of unilateral decisions. Further international agencies may need to be established in order to confront together the stewardship of this "home" of ours; more important, however, is the need for ever greater conviction about the need for responsible cooperation. The problems looming on the horizon are complex, and time is

short. In order to face this situation effectively, there is a need to act in harmony.

One area where there is a particular need to intensify dialogue between nations is that of the *stewardship of the earth's energy resources*. The technologically advanced countries are facing two pressing needs in this regard: on the one hand, to reassess the high levels of consumption due to the present model of development, and on the other hand, to invest sufficient resources in the search for alternative sources of energy and for greater energy efficiency. The emerging countries are hungry for energy, but at times this hunger is met in a way harmful to poor countries which, due to their insufficient infrastructures, including their technological infrastructures, are forced to undersell the energy resources they do possess. At times, their very political freedom is compromised by forms of protectorate or, in any case, by forms of conditioning which appear clearly humiliating.

FAMILY, HUMAN COMMUNITY AND ECONOMY

9. An essential condition for peace within individual families is that they should be built upon the solid foundation of shared spiritual and ethical values. Yet it must be added that the family experiences authentic peace when no one lacks what is needed, and when the family patrimony — the fruit of the labor of some, the savings of others, and the active cooperation of all — is well-managed in a spirit of solidarity, without extravagance and without waste. The peace of the family, then, requires an *openness to a transcendent patrimony of values,* and at the same time a concern for the prudent management of both material goods and interpersonal relationships. The failure of the latter results in

the breakdown of reciprocal trust in the face of the uncertainty threatening the future of the nuclear family.

10. Something similar must be said for that other family which is humanity as a whole. The human family, which today is increasingly unified as a result of globalization, also needs, in addition to a foundation of shared values, an economy capable of responding effectively to the requirements of a common good which is now planetary in scope. Here too, a comparison with the natural family proves helpful. Honest and straightforward relationships need to be promoted between individual persons and between peoples, thus enabling everyone to cooperate on a just and equal footing. Efforts must also be made to ensure a *prudent use of resources* and an *equitable distribution of wealth*. In particular, the aid given to poor countries must be guided by sound economic principles, avoiding forms of waste associated principally with the maintenance of expensive bureaucracies. Due account must also be taken of the moral obligation to ensure that the economy is not governed solely by the ruthless laws of instant profit, which can prove inhumane.

MODERATION IS
NEEDED[19]

The arrival in Bethlehem of the Magi from the East to adore the newborn Messiah is a sign of the manifestation of the universal King to the peoples and to all who seek the truth. It is the beginning of a movement opposed to that of Babel: from confusion to comprehension, from dispersion to reconciliation. Thus, we discern a link between Epiphany and Pentecost: if the Nativity of Christ, who is the Head, is also the Nativity of the Church, his Body, we can see the Magi as the peoples who join the remnant of Israel, foretelling the great sign of the "polyglot Church" that the Holy Spirit carried out fifty days after Easter. The faithful and tenacious love of God which is never lacking in his covenant from generation to generation is the "mystery" of which Saint Paul speaks in his letters and in the passage from the Letter to the Ephesians which has just been proclaimed: the apostle says that this mystery "was made known to me by revelation" (Eph 3:3).

This "mystery" of God's fidelity constitutes the hope of history. It is, of course, opposed by the impulses of division and tyranny that wound humanity due to sin and conflicts of selfishness. The Church in history is at the service of this "mystery" of blessing for all humanity. The Church fully carries out her mission in this mystery of God's fidelity only when she reflects the light of Christ the Lord within herself and so helps the peoples of the world on their way to peace and authentic progress. Indeed, God's Word revealed through the Prophet Isaiah still continues to apply: "darkness shall cover the earth, and thick darkness the peoples; but the Lord will arise upon you, and his glory will be seen upon you" (Is 60:2). What the

---

19 Pope Benedict XVI, Homily, January 6, 2008.

prophet proclaimed in Jerusalem was to be fulfilled in Christ's Church: "nations shall come to your light, and kings to the brightness of your rising" (Is 60:3).

With Jesus Christ, Abraham's blessing was extended to all peoples, to the universal Church as the new Israel which welcomes within her the whole of humanity. Yet, what the prophet said is also true today in many senses: "thick darkness [covers] the peoples" and our history. Indeed, it cannot be said that "globalization" is synonymous with "world order" — it is quite the opposite. Conflicts for economic supremacy and hoarding resources of energy, water, and raw materials hinder the work of all who are striving at every level to build a just and supportive world. There is a need for greater hope, which will make it possible to prefer the common good of all to the luxury of the few and the poverty of the many. "This great hope can only be God … not any god, but the God who has a human face" (*Spe Salvi*, No. 31): the God who showed himself in the Child of Bethlehem and the Crucified and Risen One.

If there is great hope, it is possible to persevere in sobriety. If true hope is lacking, happiness is sought in drunkenness, in the superfluous, in excesses, and we ruin ourselves and the world. It is then that moderation is not only an ascetic rule, but also a path of salvation for humanity. It is already obvious that only by adopting a sober lifestyle, accompanied by a serious effort for a fair distribution of riches, will it be possible to establish an order of just and sustainable development. For this reason we need people who nourish great hope and thus have great courage: the courage of the Magi, who made a long journey following a star and were able to kneel before a Child and offer him their precious gifts. We all need this courage, anchored to firm hope. May Mary obtain it for us, accompanying us on our earthly pilgrimage with her maternal protection. Amen!

As I begin my address to this assembly, I would like first of all to express to you, Mr. President, my sincere gratitude for your kind words. My thanks go also to the Secretary-General, Mr. Ban Ki-moon, for inviting me to visit the headquarters of this organization and for the welcome that he has extended to me. I greet the ambassadors and diplomats from the member states, and all those present. Through you, I greet the peoples who are represented here. They look to this institution to carry forward the founding inspiration to establish a "center for harmonizing the actions of nations in the attainment of these common ends" of peace and development (cf. *Charter of the United Nations*, article 1.2-1.4). As Pope John Paul II expressed it in 1995, the Organization should be "a moral center where all the nations of the world feel at home and develop a shared awareness of being, as it were, a 'family of nations'" (*Address to the General Assembly of the United Nations on the 50th Anniversary of its Foundation*, New York, October 5, 1995, No. 14).

Through the United Nations, states have established universal objectives which, even if they do not coincide with the total common good of the human family, undoubtedly represent a fundamental part of that good. The founding principles of the organization — the desire for peace, the quest for justice, respect for the dignity of the person, humanitarian cooperation and assistance — express the just aspirations of the human spirit, and constitute the ideals which should underpin international relations. As my predecessors Paul VI and John Paul II have observed from this very podium, all this is something that the Catholic Church and the Holy See follow attentively and with interest,

---

20 Pope Benedict XVI, Address at the Meeting with the Members of the General Assembly of the United Nations Organization, New York, April 18, 2008.

seeing in your activity an example of how issues and conflicts concerning the world community can be subject to common regulation.

The United Nations embodies the aspiration for a "greater degree of international ordering" (John Paul II, *Sollicitudo Rei Socialis*, No. 43), inspired and governed by the principle of subsidiarity, and therefore capable of responding to the demands of the human family through binding international rules and through structures capable of harmonizing the day-to-day unfolding of the lives of peoples. This is all the more necessary at a time when we experience the obvious paradox of a multilateral consensus that continues to be in crisis because it is still subordinated to the decisions of a few, whereas the world's problems call for interventions in the form of collective action by the international community.

Indeed, questions of security, development goals, reduction of local and global inequalities, protection of the environment, of resources and of the climate, require all international leaders to act jointly and to show a readiness to work in good faith, respecting the law, and promoting solidarity with the weakest regions of the planet. I am thinking especially of those countries in Africa and other parts of the world which remain on the margins of authentic integral development, and are therefore at risk of experiencing only the negative effects of globalization. In the context of international relations, it is necessary to recognize the higher role played by rules and structures that are intrinsically ordered to promote the common good, and therefore to safeguard human freedom. These regulations do not limit freedom. On the contrary, they promote it when they prohibit behavior and actions which work against the common good, curb its effective exercise, and hence compromise the dignity of every human person.

In the name of freedom, there has to be a correlation between rights and duties, by which every person is called to assume responsibility for his or her choices, made as a consequence of entering into relations with others. Here our thoughts turn also to the way the results of scientific research and technological advances have sometimes been applied. Notwithstanding the enormous benefits that humanity can gain, some instances of this represent a clear violation of the order of creation, to the point where not only is the sacred character of life contradicted, but the human person and the family are robbed of their natural identity. Likewise, international action to preserve the environment and to protect various forms of life on earth must not only guarantee a rational use of technology and science, but must also rediscover the authentic image of creation. This never requires a choice to be made between science and ethics: rather it is a question of adopting a scientific method that is truly respectful of ethical imperatives.

Recognition of the unity of the human family, and attention to the innate dignity of every man and woman, today find renewed emphasis in the principle of the responsibility to protect. This has only recently been defined, but it was already present implicitly at the origins of the United Nations, and is now increasingly characteristic of its activity. Every state has the primary duty to protect its own population from grave and sustained violations of human rights, as well as from the consequences of humanitarian crises, whether natural or man-made. If states are unable to guarantee such protection, the international community must intervene with the juridical means provided in the United Nations Charter and in other international instruments. The action of the international community and its institutions, provided that it respects the principles undergirding the international order, should never be interpreted as an unwarranted imposition or a limitation of sovereignty. On the contrary, it is indifference or failure to intervene that do the real damage. What is needed is a deeper search for ways of pre-empting and managing conflicts by exploring every possible diplomatic avenue, and giving attention and encouragement to even the faintest sign of dialogue or desire for reconciliation.

The principle of "responsibility to protect" was considered by the ancient *ius gentium* as the foundation of every action taken by those in government with regard to the governed: at the time when the concept of national sovereign states was first developing, the Dominican Friar Francisco de Vitoria, rightly considered as a precursor of the idea of the United Nations, described this responsibility as an aspect of natural reason shared by all nations, and the result of an international order whose task it was to regulate relations between peoples. Now, as then, this principle has to invoke the idea of the person as image of the Creator, the desire for the absolute and the essence of freedom.

The founding of the United Nations, as we know, coincided with the profound upheavals that humanity experienced when reference to the meaning of transcendence and natural reason was abandoned, and in consequence, freedom and human dignity were grossly violated. When this happens, it threatens the objective foundations of the values inspiring and governing the international order and it undermines the cogent and inviolable principles formulated and consolidated by the United Nations. When faced with new and insistent challenges, it is a mistake to fall back on a pragmatic approach, limited to determining "common ground," minimal in content and weak in its effect.

This reference to human dignity, which is the foundation and goal of the responsibility to protect, leads us to the theme we are specifically focusing upon this year, which marks the sixtieth anniversary of the *Universal Declaration of Human Rights*. This document was the outcome of a convergence of different religious and cultural traditions, all of them motivated by the common desire to place the human person at the heart of institutions, laws, and the workings of society, and to consider the human person essential for the world of culture, religion, and science. Human rights are increasingly being presented as the common language and the ethical substratum of international relations. At the same time, the universality, indivisibility, and interdependence of human rights all serve as guarantees safeguarding human dignity.

It is evident, though, that the rights recognized and expounded in the *Declaration* apply to everyone by virtue of the common origin of the person, who remains the high point of God's creative design for the world and for history. They are based on the natural law inscribed on human hearts and present in different cultures and civilizations. Removing human rights from this context would mean restricting their range and yielding to a relativistic conception, according to which the meaning and interpretation of rights could vary and their universality would be denied in the name of different cultural, political, social, and even religious outlooks. This great variety of viewpoints must not be allowed to obscure the fact that not only rights are universal, but so too is the human person, the subject of those rights....

My presence at this assembly is a sign of esteem for the United Nations, and it is intended to express the hope that the organization will increasingly serve as a sign of unity between states and an instrument of service to the entire human family. It also demonstrates the willingness of the Catholic Church to offer her proper contribution to building international relations in a way that allows every person and every people to feel they can make a difference. In a manner that is consistent with her contribution in the ethical and moral sphere and the free activity of her faithful, the Church also works for the realization of these goals through the international activity of the Holy See. Indeed, the Holy See has always had a place at the assemblies of the Nations, thereby manifesting its specific character as a subject in the international domain. As the United Nations recently confirmed, the Holy See thereby makes its contribution according to the dispositions of international law, helps to define that law, and makes appeal to it.

The United Nations remains a privileged setting in which the Church is committed to contributing her experience "of humanity," developed over the centuries among peoples of every race and culture, and placing it at the disposal of all members of the international community. This experience and activity, directed toward attaining freedom for every believer, seeks also to increase the protection given to the rights of the person. Those rights are grounded and shaped by the transcendent nature of the person, which permits men and women to pursue their journey of faith and their search for God in this world. Recognition of this dimension must be strengthened if we are to sustain humanity's hope for a better world and if we are to create the conditions for peace, development, cooperation, and guarantee of rights for future generations.

In my Encyclical *Spe Salvi*, I indicated that "every generation has the task of engaging anew in the arduous search for the right way to order human affairs" (No. 25). For Christians, this task is motivated by the hope drawn from the saving work of Jesus

Christ. That is why the Church is happy to be associated with the activity of this distinguished organization, charged with the responsibility of promoting peace and good will throughout the earth. Dear Friends, I thank you for this opportunity to address you today, and I promise you of the support of my prayers as you pursue your noble task.

Before I take my leave from this distinguished assembly, I should like to offer my greetings, in the official languages, to all the Nations here represented.

Peace and prosperity with God's help!

Subsidiarity and Solidarity[21]

This year, for your customary gathering, you have chosen the theme: "Social capital and human development." You have paused to reflect on the need, felt by many, to promote a global development aimed at the integral promotion of man, also highlighting the contribution that volunteer associations can give, such as nonprofit foundations and other types of community entities that have been founded with the goal of making the social fabric ever more solid. A harmonious development is possible if the economic and political choices take into account and put into practice those fundamental principles which make it accessible to all. I am referring, in particular, to the principles of subsidiarity and solidarity. It is always necessary that the person, created in the image of God and willed by him to keep and administer the immense resources of creation, be at the center of every economic program, especially considering the vast and complex network of relations which characterize the postmodern epoch. Only a shared culture of responsible and active participation can enable each human being to feel not as a consumer or a passive bystander, but an active collaborator in the process of world development.

Man, to whom, in Genesis, God entrusted the earth, has the duty to make all the earth's goods fruitful, committing himself to use them to satisfy the multiple needs of each member of the human family. One of the recurring metaphors of the Gospel is, in effect, exactly that of the steward. With the heart of a faithful administrator man must, therefore, administer the resources entrusted to him by God, putting them at the disposition of all. In other words, one must avoid that the profit accrue only to the individual or that forms of collectivism oppress personal freedom.

---

21 Pope Benedict XVI, Address to Members of the "*Centesimus Annus — Pro Pontifice*" Foundation, May 31, 2008.

Economic or commercial interests must never become exclusive, because, indeed, this would be to mortify human dignity.

Since the process of globalization, taking place in the world, invests ever more in the field of culture, economics, finance, and politics, the great challenge today is "to globalize" not only economic and commercial interests, but also the expectations of solidarity, with respect for and valuing the contribution of each component of society. As you have opportunely confirmed, economic growth must never be separate from seeking integral human and social development. In this regard, the Church, in her social doctrine, emphasizes the importance of the contribution of intermediate bodies according to the principle of subsidiarity, to freely contribute to orient cultural and social changes and to direct them to the authentic progress of the person and the community. In the Encyclical *Spe Salvi*, I had purposely reaffirmed that "the best structures function only when the community is animated by convictions capable of motivating people to assent freely to the social order" (No. 24).

Dear friends, while I renew my gratitude for the generous support that you untiringly lend to charitable activities and to the human promotion of the Church, I invite you also to offer the contribution of your reflection to bring about a just economic world order. In this regard, I am pleased to cite an eloquent affirmation of the Second Vatican Council: "Christians," one reads in the Constitution *Gaudium et Spes,* "can yearn for nothing more ardently than to serve the men of this age with an ever growing generosity and success. Holding loyally to the Gospel, enriched by its resources, and joining forces with all who love and practice justice, they have shouldered a weighty task here on earth" (No. 93). Continue your action in this spirit to help so many of our brothers and sisters. On the Last Day, on the Day of the Universal Judgment, we will be asked if we have used what God has put at our disposition to meet the legitimate expectations and needs of our brethren, especially the smallest and neediest.

May the Virgin Mary, whom we contemplate today on her visit to her cousin Elizabeth, obtain for each one of you an ever greater concern for your neighbor. I assure you of a remembrance in prayer and with affection I impart my apostolic blessing to you present here, to your families, and to those who collaborate with you in your various professional activities.

WISE USE OF RESOURCES[22]

Another challenge for Guatemala is that of remedying the malnutrition of many children. The right to nutrition responds principally to an ethical motivation: "give the hungry to eat" (cf. Mt 25:35), that prompts a sharing of material goods as a sign of the love which we all need. As I have already stated on another occasion: "The objective of eradicating hunger and at the same time of being able to count on healthy and adequate food also demands specific methods and actions that mean a wise use of resources that respect Creation's patrimony." Working in this direction is a priority that will benefit not only science, research, and technology, but also take into account the cycles and rhythm of nature known to the inhabitants of rural areas, thus protecting the traditional customs of the indigenous communities, leaving aside egotistical and exclusively economic motivations (cf. *Message to the Director General of FAO on the occasion of the World Food Day,* October 4, 2007).

---

22 Pope Benedict XVI, Address, May 31, 2008.

I am pleased to address my respectful and cordial greeting to you, who, in different capacities, represent the various components of the human family and are gathered in Rome to negotiate suitable solutions to face the problem of hunger and malnutrition.

I have asked Cardinal Tarcisio Bertone, my Secretary of State, to express to you the particular attention with which I am following your work and assure you that I attribute great importance to the arduous duty that awaits you. Millions of men and women look to you while new snares threaten their survival and worrisome situations put the security of their nations at risk. In fact, the growing globalization of markets does not always favor the availability of foodstuffs and the systems of production are often conditioned by structural limits, not to mention by political protection and speculative phenomena that relegate entire populations to the margins of development processes. In light of this situation, one must strongly repeat that hunger and malnutrition are unacceptable in a world that, in reality, possesses production levels, resources, and sufficient knowledge to put an end to these dramas and their consequences. The great challenge of today is "'to globalize' not only economic and commercial interests, but also the expectations of solidarity, with respect for and valuing the contribution of each component of society" (cf. *Address to the Centesimus Annus — Pro Pontifice Foundation*, May 31, 2008).

To the FAO and to its Director General, therefore, go my appreciation and my gratitude, for having again drawn the international community's attention to what obstructs the fight

---

23 Pope Benedict XVI, Message to Participants Attending the "High-Level Conference on World Food Security: The Challenges of Climate Change and Bioenergy," Organized by the United Nations' Food and Agriculture Organization, June 2, 2008.

against hunger and for having solicited it to take action, an action that must be united and coordinated in order to be effective.

In this spirit, to the high-level personages participating in this summit I should like to renew the wish that I expressed during my recent visit to the U.N. headquarters: it is urgent to overcome the "paradox of a multilateral consensus that continues to be in crisis because it is still subordinated to the decisions of a few" (*Address to United Nations' General Assembly*, April 18, 2008). Furthermore, may I invite you to cooperate in an ever more transparent manner with the organizations of civil society committed to filling the growing gap between wealth and poverty. Again I exhort you to continue with those structural reforms that, on a national level, are indispensable to successfully confront the problems of underdevelopment, of which hunger and malnutrition are direct consequences. I know how arduous and complex it all is!

Yet, how can one remain insensitive to the appeals of those who, on the various continents, are not able to feed themselves enough to live? Poverty and malnutrition are not a mere fatality caused by adverse environmental circumstances or by disastrous natural calamities. On the other hand, considerations of an exclusively technical or economic character must not prevail over the rights of justice toward those who suffer from hunger. "The right to nutrition responds principally to an ethical motivation: 'give the hungry to eat' (cf. Mt 25: 35), that prompts a sharing of material goods as a sign of the love which we all need.... This primary right to nutrition is intrinsically linked to the safeguarding and to the defense of human life, the solid and inviolable rock upon which the whole edifice of human rights is founded" (*Address to the New Ambassador of Guatemala*, May 31, 2008). Each person has the right to life: therefore it is necessary to promote the effective actualization of such rights, and the populations that suffer from lack of food must be helped to gradually become capable of satisfying their own needs for sufficient and healthy nutrition.

At this particular moment, in which food security is threatened by the rise in price of agricultural products, new strategies need to be worked out in the fight against poverty and the promotion of rural development. This must also happen through structural-reform processes that would enable the challenges of the same security and of climatic changes to be faced. Furthermore, it is necessary to increase the food available by promoting industrious small farmers and guaranteeing them access to the market. The global increase in the production of agricultural products, however, can be effective only if production is accompanied by effective distribution and if it is primarily destined to satisfy essential needs. It certainly is not easy, but it would allow, among other things, to rediscover the value of the rural family: it would not be limited to preserving the transmission, from parents to children, of the cultivation methods, of conserving and distributing foodstuffs, but above all it would preserve a model of life, of education, of culture, and of religiosity. Moreover, from the economic profile, it ensures an effective and loving attention to the weakest and, by virtue of the principle of subsidiarity, it could assume a direct role in the distribution chain and the trading of agricultural food products reducing the costs of intermediaries and favoring small-scale production.

Ladies and Gentlemen,

Today's difficulties show how modern technology by itself is not sufficient to provide for the lack of food, neither are statistical calculations nor, in emergency situations, the sending of food supplies. All this certainly has a great impact, yet it must be completed and oriented to a political action that, inspired by those principles of the natural law which are written on the human heart, protect the dignity of the person. In this way, also the order of Creation is respected and one has "the good of all as a constant guiding criterion" (*Message for the World Day of Peace,* January 1, 2008, No. 7). Hence, only by protecting the person is it possible to overcome the main causes of hunger, such as being closed to one's neighbor which dissolves solidarity, justifies models of consumeristic life, and unravels the social fabric, preserving, if not actually deepening, the furrows of unjust balances and neglecting the most profound demands of good (cf. *Deus Caritas Est,* No. 28).

If, therefore, respect for human dignity were given its worth on the negotiation table, in making decisions and accomplishing them, it would be possible to rise above otherwise insurmountable obstacles, and it would eliminate, or at least diminish, the disinterest in the good of others. Consequently, it would be possible to adopt courageous measures that would not stop before hunger and malnutrition, as if they were simply considered unsolvable, endemic phenomena. It could help if, in the defense of human dignity, international action — even emergency action — were to estimate the superfluous in the perspective of the needs of others and to administer the fruit of Creation according to justice, placing it at the disposition of all generations.

In the light of these principles, I hope that the delegations present at this meeting will take on new commitments and be resolved to accomplish them with great determination. The Catholic Church, for her part, desires to join in these efforts! In a spirit of collaboration, drawing on ancient wisdom, inspired by the Gospel, she makes a firm and heartfelt appeal that is very relevant for those participating in the summit: "Give to eat to the one who is starving of hunger, because, if you do not give to him to eat, you will kill him" (cf. *Decretum Gratiani,* c. 21, d. LXXXVI). I assure you that, along this path, you can count on the support of the Holy See. Although it differentiates itself from states, it is united to their most noble objectives to seal a commitment that, by her nature, involves the entire international community: to encourage every people to share the needs of other peoples, placing in common the goods of the earth that the Creator has destined for the entire human family. With these sentiments, I express my most fervent wishes for the success of your work and invoke the blessing of the Most High upon you and upon those who are committed to the authentic progress of the person and of society.

WONDROUS VIEW OF
THE WORLD[24]

Almost two thousand years ago, the apostles, gathered in the Upper Room together with Mary and some faithful women, were filled with the Holy Spirit (cf. Acts 1:14; 2:4). At that extraordinary moment, which gave birth to the Church, the confusion and fear that had gripped Christ's disciples were transformed into a vigorous conviction and sense of purpose. They felt impelled to speak of their encounter with the risen Jesus whom they had come to call affectionately, the Lord. In many ways, the apostles were ordinary. None could claim to be the perfect disciple. They failed to recognize Christ (cf. Lk 24:13-32), felt ashamed of their own ambition (cf. Lk 22:24-27), and had even denied him (cf. Lk 22:54-62). Yet, when empowered by the Holy Spirit, they were transfixed by the truth of Christ's Gospel and inspired to proclaim it fearlessly. Emboldened, they exclaimed: repent, be baptized, receive the Holy Spirit (cf. Acts 2:37-38)!

Grounded in the apostles' teaching, in fellowship, and in the breaking of the bread and prayer (cf. Acts 2:42), the young Christian community moved forward to oppose the perversity in the culture around them (cf. Acts 2:40), to care for one another (cf. Acts 2:44-47), to defend their belief in Jesus in the face of hostility (cf. Acts 4:33), and to heal the sick (cf. Acts 5:12-16). And in obedience to Christ's own command, they set forth, bearing witness to the greatest story ever: that God has become one of us, that the divine has entered human history in order to transform it, and that we are called to immerse ourselves in Christ's saving love which triumphs over evil and death. Saint Paul, in his famous speech to the Areopagus, introduced the message in this

---

24 Pope Benedict XVI, Address, Welcoming Celebration by Young People for World Youth Day in Sydney, Australia, July 17, 2008.

way: "God gives everything — including life and breath — to everyone ... so that all nations might seek God and, by feeling their way towards him, succeed in finding him. In fact he is not far from any of us, since it is in him that we live and move and have our being" (Acts 17:25-28).

And ever since, men and women have set out to tell the same story, witnessing to Christ's truth and love, and contributing to the Church's mission. Today, we think of those pioneering priests, sisters, and brothers who came to these shores, and to other parts of the Pacific, from Ireland, France, Britain, and elsewhere in Europe. The great majority were young — some still in their late teens — and when they bade farewell to their parents, brothers and sisters, and friends, they knew they were unlikely ever to return home. Their whole lives were a selfless Christian witness. They became the humble but tenacious builders of so much of the social and spiritual heritage which still today brings goodness, compassion, and purpose to these nations. And they went on to inspire another generation. We think immediately of the faith which sustained Blessed Mary MacKillop in her sheer determination to educate especially the poor, and Blessed Peter To Rot in his steadfast resolution that community leadership must always include the Gospel. Think also of your own grandparents and parents, your first teachers in faith. They too have made countless sacrifices of time and energy, out of love for you. Supported by your parish priests and teachers, they have the task, not always easy but greatly satisfying, of guiding you toward all that is good and true, through their own witness — their teaching and living of our Christian faith.

Today, it is my turn. For some of us, it might seem like we have come to the end of the world! For people of your age, however, any flight is an exciting prospect. But for me, this one was somewhat daunting! Yet the views afforded of our planet from the air were truly wondrous. The sparkle of the Mediterranean, the grandeur of the north African desert, the lushness of Asia's forestation, the vastness of the Pacific Ocean, the horizon upon which the sun rose and set, and the majestic splendor of Australia's natural beauty which I have been able to enjoy these last couple of days; these all evoke a profound sense of awe. It is as though one catches glimpses of the Genesis creation story — light and darkness, the sun and the moon, the waters, the earth, and living creatures; all of which are "good" in God's eyes (cf. Gn 1:1—2:4). Immersed in such beauty, who could not echo the words of the Psalmist in praise of the Creator: "how majestic is your name in all the earth?" (Ps 8:1).

And there is more — something hardly perceivable from the sky — men and women, made in nothing less than God's own image and likeness (cf. Gn 1:26). At the heart of the marvel of creation are you and I, the human family "crowned with glory and honor" (Ps 8:5). How astounding! With the Psalmist we whisper: "what is man that you are mindful of him?" (Ps 8:4). And drawn into silence, into a spirit of thanksgiving, into the power of holiness, we ponder.

What do we discover? Perhaps reluctantly we come to acknowledge that there are also scars which mark the surface of our earth: erosion, deforestation, the squandering of the world's mineral and ocean resources in order to fuel an insatiable consumption. Some of you come from island nations whose very existence is threatened by rising water levels; others from nations suffering the effects of devastating drought. God's wondrous creation is sometimes experienced as almost hostile to its stewards, even something dangerous. How can what is "good" appear so threatening?

And there is more. What of man, the apex of God's creation? Every day we encounter the genius of human achievement. From advances in medical sciences and the wise application of technology, to the creativity reflected in the arts, the quality and enjoyment of people's lives in many ways are steadily rising. Among yourselves there is a readiness to take up the plentiful opportunities offered to you. Some of you excel in studies, sport, music, or dance and drama, others of you have a keen sense of social justice and ethics, and many of you take up service and voluntary work. All of us, young and old, have those moments when the innate goodness of the human person — perhaps glimpsed in the gesture of a little child or an adult's readiness to forgive — fills us with profound joy and gratitude....

My dear friends, God's creation is one and it is good. The concerns for nonviolence, sustainable development, justice and peace, and care for our environment are of vital importance for humanity. They cannot, however, be understood apart from a profound reflection upon the innate dignity of every human life from conception to natural death: a dignity conferred by God himself and thus inviolable. Our world has grown weary of greed, exploitation, and division, of the tedium of false idols and piecemeal responses, and the pain of false promises. Our hearts and minds are yearning for a vision of life where love endures, where gifts are shared, where unity is built, where freedom finds meaning in truth, and where identity is found in respectful communion. This is the work of the Holy Spirit! This is the hope held out by the Gospel of Jesus Christ. It is to bear witness to this reality, that you were created anew at baptism and strengthened through the gifts of the Spirit at confirmation. Let this be the message that you bring from Sydney to the world!

CHALLENGES OF CLIMATE CHANGE[25]

The theme chosen this year for Word Food Day, *"World Food Security: the Challenges of Climate Change and Bioenergy,"* permits a reflection on what has been achieved in the fight against hunger and on the obstacles to the action of the Food and Agriculture Organization of the United Nations (FAO) in the face of new challenges that threaten the life of the human family.

This day is being celebrated at a particularly difficult time for the world nutritional situation, when the availability of food seems inadequate in relation to consumption and climate change contributes to endangering the survival of millions of men, women, and children, forced to leave their country in search of food. These circumstances mean that, together with the FAO, everyone must respond in terms of solidarity with actions free from all conditioning and truly at the service of the common good.

Last June, the *High-Level Conference on Word Food Security* afforded the FAO an opportunity to remind the international community of its direct responsibilities for food insecurity while basic aid for emergency situations risks being limited. In the message I addressed to the participants at the time I pointed out the need "to adopt courageous measures, that would not stop before hunger and malnutrition, as if they simply concerned unsolvable, endemic phenomena" (*Message of the Holy Father*, June 2, 2008, read by Cardinal Tarcisio Bertone, Secretary of State, at the headquarters of the FAO, Rome, on that date).

The first task is to eliminate the causes that prevent authentic respect for the person's dignity. The means and resources of which the world disposes today can procure sufficient food to

---

25 Pope Benedict XVI, Message to the General Director of the Food and Agriculture Organization of the United Nations, October 13, 2008.

satisfy the growing needs of all. This has been demonstrated by the first results of the effort to increase global production levels in the face of the shortage recorded in recent harvests. So why is it not possible to prevent so many people suffering the most extreme consequences of hunger? There are numerous reasons for this situation in which abundance and a deficit often coexist. Thus one can mention the food race that does not stop in spite of the constantly diminishing supply of foodstuffs which imposes reductions on the nutritional capacity of the poorest regions of the world, or the lack of determination to conclude negotiations and to check the selfishness of states and groups of countries, or further, to put an end to that "unbridled speculation" which affects the mechanisms of prices and consumption. The absence of a correct administration of food resources caused by corruption in public life or growing investments in weapons and sophisticated military technology to the detriment of the primary needs of people also plays an important role.

These very different reasons originate in a false sense of the values on which international relations should be based and, in particular, in the widespread attitude in contemporary culture which gives exclusive priority to the race for material goods, forgetting the true nature of the human person and his deepest aspirations. Unfortunately, the result is the inability of many to take charge of the needs of the poor and to understand them, and the denial of their inalienable dignity. An effective campaign against hunger thus demands far more than a mere scientific study to confront climate change or give priority to the agricultural production of food. It is necessary first of all to rediscover the meaning of the human person, in his individual and community dimensions, from the founding of family life, a source of love and affection from which the sense of solidarity and sharing develop. This setting satisfies the need to build relations between peoples, based on constant and authentic availability, to enable each country to satisfy the requirements of needy people but also to transmit the idea of relations based on a reciprocal exchange of knowledge, values, rapid assistance, and respect.

This commitment to promoting effective social justice in international relations demands of each one an awareness that the goods of creation are destined for all, and that in the world community economies must be oriented toward the sharing of these goods, their lasting use, and the fair division of the benefits that derive from them.

In the changing context of international relations, where uncertainties seem to be growing and new challenges are glimpsed, the experience acquired to date by the FAO alongside that of other institutions active in the fight against hunger can play a fundamental role in promoting a new way of understanding international cooperation. One essential condition for increasing production levels, for guaranteeing the identity of indigenous communities as well as peace and security in the world, is to guarantee access to land, thereby favoring farmworkers and upholding their rights.

The Catholic Church is close to you in all these efforts. This is testified by the attention with which the Holy See has followed the activity of the FAO since 1948, constantly supporting your endeavors so that your commitment to the cause of the human being might be pursued. This means, in practice, openness to life, respect for the order of Creation, and adherence to the ethical principles that have always been the basis of social life.

With these wishes, I invoke upon you, Mr. Director General, as well as upon all the representatives of the nations, the blessing of the Most High, that you may work generously with a sense of justice for the most neglected peoples.

The gap between rich and poor has become more marked, even in the most economically developed nations. This is a problem which the conscience of humanity cannot ignore, since the conditions in which a great number of people are living are an insult to their innate dignity and as a result are a threat to the authentic and harmonious progress of the world community" (*Message for the 1993 World Day of Peace,* No. 1).

2. In this context, fighting poverty requires *attentive consideration of the complex phenomenon of globalization.* This is important from a methodological standpoint, because it suggests drawing upon the fruits of economic and sociological research into the many different aspects of poverty. Yet the reference to globalization should also alert us to the spiritual and moral implications of the question, urging us, in our dealings with the poor, to set out from the clear recognition that we all share in a single divine plan: we are called to form one family in which all — individuals, peoples, and nations — model their behavior according to the principles of fraternity and responsibility.

This perspective requires an understanding of poverty that is wide-ranging and well articulated. If it were a question of material poverty alone, then the social sciences, which enable us to measure phenomena on the basis of mainly quantitative data, would be sufficient to illustrate its principal characteristics. Yet we know that other, nonmaterial forms of poverty exist which are not the direct and automatic consequence of material deprivation. For example, in advanced wealthy societies, there is evi-

---

26 Pope Benedict XVI, Message for the Celebration of the World Day of Peace, January 1, 2009.

dence of *marginalization,* as well as *affective, moral, and spiritual poverty,* seen in people whose interior lives are disoriented and who experience various forms of malaise despite their economic prosperity. On the one hand, I have in mind what is known as "moral underdevelopment" (Paul VI, *Populorum Progressio,* No. 19), and on the other hand the negative consequences of "superdevelopment" (John Paul II, *Sollicitudo Rei Socialis,* No. 28). Nor can I forget that, in so-called poor societies, economic growth is often hampered by *cultural impediments* which lead to inefficient use of available resources. It remains true, however, that every form of externally imposed poverty has at its root a lack of respect for the transcendent dignity of the human person. When man is not considered within the total context of his vocation, and when the demands of a true "human ecology" (John Paul II, *Centesimus Annus,* No. 38) are not respected, the cruel forces of poverty are unleashed, as is evident in certain specific areas that I shall now consider briefly one by one.

It is toward the poor, the all too many poor people on our planet, that I would like to turn my attention today, taking up my *Message for the World Day of Peace*, devoted this year to the theme: "Fighting Poverty to Build Peace." The insightful analysis of Pope Paul VI in the Encyclical *Populorum Progressio* has lost none of its timeliness: "Today we see people trying to secure a sure food supply, cures for disease, and steady employment. We see them trying to eliminate every ill, to remove every obstacle which offends man's dignity. They are constantly striving to exercise greater personal responsibility; to do more, to learn more and to have more, in order to be more. And yet, at the same time, so many people continue to live in conditions which frustrate these legitimate desires" (No. 6).

To build peace, we need to give new hope to the poor. How can we not think of so many individuals and families hard-pressed by the difficulties and uncertainties which the current financial and economic crisis has provoked on a global scale? How can we not mention the food crisis and global warming, which make it even more difficult for those living in some of the poorest parts of the planet to have access to nutrition and water? There is an urgent need to adopt an effective strategy to fight hunger and to promote local agricultural development, all the more so since the number of the poor is increasing even within the rich countries. In this perspective, I am pleased that the recent Doha Conference on financing development identified some helpful criteria for directing the governance of the economic system and helping those who are most in need.

On a deeper level, bolstering the economy demands rebuilding confidence. This goal will only be reached by implementing

---

27 Pope Benedict XVI, Address, January 8, 2009.

an ethics based on the innate dignity of the human person. I know how demanding this will be, yet it is not a utopia! Today, more than in the past, our future is at stake, as well as the fate of our planet and its inhabitants, especially the younger generation which is inheriting a severely compromised economic system and social fabric.

FAIR DISTRIBUTION OF RESOURCES[28]

The United Nations Conference on the economic and financial crisis and on its impact on development is to be held June 24-26 in New York. I invoke the spirit of wisdom and human solidarity upon the participants in the conference, as well as on those responsible for public affairs and for the future of the planet, so that the current crisis may be turned into an opportunity that is capable of focusing greater attention on the dignity of every human person and of promoting a fair distribution of decision-making power and resources, with special attention to the number of poor people, which is unfortunately constantly increasing.

On this day, on which Italy and many other nations celebrate the *feast of Corpus Christi,* the "Bread of Life," as I have just said, I would like to remember in particular the hundreds of millions of people who are suffering from hunger. This is an absolutely unacceptable situation that even after the efforts of recent decades is proving difficult to reduce. I therefore hope that on the occasion of the upcoming U.N. conference, and at the headquarters of international institutions, provisions shared by the whole of the international community will be made, as well as strategic decisions, sometimes far from easy to accept but which are necessary in order to assure basic foodstuffs and a dignified life to one and all, in the present and in the future.

---

28 Pope Benedict XVI, Angelus, June 14, 2009.

21. [Pope] Paul VI had an *articulated vision of development*. He understood the term to indicate the goal of rescuing peoples, first and foremost, from hunger, deprivation, endemic diseases, and illiteracy. From the economic point of view, this meant their active participation, on equal terms, in the international economic process; from the social point of view, it meant their evolution into educated societies marked by solidarity; from the political point of view, it meant the consolidation of democratic regimes capable of ensuring freedom and peace. After so many years, as we observe with concern the developments and perspectives of the succession of crises that afflict the world today, *we ask to what extent Paul VI's expectations have been fulfilled* by the model of development adopted in recent decades. We recognize, therefore, that the Church had good reason to be concerned about the capacity of a purely technological society to set realistic goals and to make good use of the instruments at its disposal.

Profit is useful if it serves as a means toward an end that provides a sense both of how to produce it and how to make good use of it. Once profit becomes the exclusive goal, if it is produced by improper means and without the common good as its ultimate end, it risks destroying wealth and creating poverty. The economic development that Paul VI hoped to see was meant to produce real growth, of benefit to everyone and genuinely sustainable. It is true that growth has taken place, and it continues to be a positive factor that has lifted billions of people out of misery — recently it has given many countries the possibility of becoming effective players in international politics. Yet it must be acknowledged that this same economic growth has been and continues to be weighed down by *malfunctions and*

---

29 Pope Benedict XVI, Encyclical Letter *Caritas in Veritate* ("In Charity and Truth"), June 29, 2009.

dramatic problems, highlighted even further by the current crisis. This presents us with choices that cannot be postponed concerning nothing less than the destiny of man, who, moreover, cannot prescind from his nature.

The technical forces in play, the global interrelations, the damaging effects on the real economy of badly managed and largely speculative financial dealing, large-scale migration of peoples, often provoked by some particular circumstance and then given insufficient attention, the unregulated exploitation of the earth's resources: all this leads us today to reflect on the measures that would be necessary to provide a solution to problems that are not only new in comparison to those addressed by Pope Paul VI, but also, and above all, of decisive impact upon the present and future good of humanity.

The different aspects of the crisis, its solutions, and any new development that the future may bring, are increasingly interconnected, they imply one another, they require new efforts of holistic understanding and a *new humanistic synthesis*. The complexity and gravity of the present economic situation rightly cause us concern, but we must adopt a realistic attitude as we take up with confidence and hope the new responsibilities to which we are called by the prospect of a world in need of profound cultural renewal, a world that needs to rediscover fundamental values on which to build a better future. The current crisis obliges us to re-plan our journey, to set ourselves new rules and to discover new forms of commitment, to build on positive experiences and to reject negative ones. The crisis thus becomes *an opportunity for discernment, in which to shape a new vision for the future.* In this spirit, with confidence rather than resignation, it is appropriate to address the difficulties of the present time.

22. Today the picture of development has *many overlapping layers*. The actors and the causes in both underdevelopment and development are manifold, the faults and the merits are differentiated. This fact should prompt us to liberate ourselves from ideologies, which often oversimplify reality in artificial ways, and it should lead us to examine objectively the full human dimension of the problems. As John Paul II has already observed, the demarcation line between rich and poor countries is no longer as clear as it was at the time of *Populorum Progressio* (cf. *Sollicitudo Rei Socialis*, No. 28). *The world's wealth is growing in absolute terms, but inequalities are on the increase*. In rich countries, new sectors of society are succumbing to poverty and new forms of poverty are emerging. In poorer areas some groups enjoy a sort of "superdevelopment" of a wasteful and consumerist kind which forms an unacceptable contrast with the ongoing situations of dehumanizing deprivation. "The scandal of glaring inequalities" (Paul VI, *Populorum Progressio*, No. 9) continues.

Corruption and illegality are unfortunately evident in the conduct of the economic and political class in rich countries, both old and new, as well as in poor ones. Among those who sometimes fail to respect the human rights of workers are large multinational companies as well as local producers. International aid has often been diverted from its proper ends, through irresponsible actions both within the chain of donors and within that of the beneficiaries. Similarly, in the context of immaterial or cultural causes of development and underdevelopment, we find these same patterns of responsibility reproduced. On the part of rich countries there is excessive zeal for protecting knowledge through an unduly rigid assertion of the right to intellectual property, especially in the field of health care. At the same time, in some poor countries, cultural models and social norms of behavior persist which hinder the process of development.

23. Many areas of the globe today have evolved considerably, albeit in problematical and disparate ways, thereby taking their place among the great powers destined to play important roles in the future. Yet it should be stressed that *progress of a merely economic and technological kind is insufficient.* Development needs above all to be true and integral. The mere fact of emerging from economic backwardness, though positive in itself, does not resolve the complex issues of human advancement, neither for the countries that are spearheading such progress, nor for those that are already economically developed, nor even for those that are still poor, which can suffer not just through old forms of exploitation, but also from the negative consequences of a growth that is marked by irregularities and imbalances.

After the collapse of the economic and political systems of the Communist countries of Eastern Europe and the end of the so-called *opposing blocs,* a complete re-examination of development was needed. Pope John Paul II called for it, when in 1987 he pointed to the existence of these blocs as one of the principal causes of underdevelopment (cf. *Sollicitudo Rei Socialis,* No. 20), inasmuch as politics withdrew resources from the economy and from the culture, and ideology inhibited freedom. Moreover, in 1991, after the events of 1989, he asked that, in view of the ending of the blocs, there should be a comprehensive new plan for development, not only in those countries, but also in the West and in those parts of the world that were in the process of evolving (cf. John Paul II, *Centesimus Annus,* Nos. 22-29). This has been achieved only in part, and it is still a real duty that needs to be discharged, perhaps by means of the choices that are necessary to overcome current economic problems.

24. The world that Paul VI had before him — even though society had already evolved to such an extent that he could speak of social issues in global terms — was still far less integrated than today's world. Economic activity and the political process were both largely conducted within the same geographical area, and could therefore feed off one another. Production took place predominantly within national boundaries, and financial investments had somewhat limited circulation outside the country, so that the politics of many states could still determine the priorities of the economy and to some degree govern its performance using the instruments at their disposal. Hence *Populorum Progressio* assigned a central, albeit not exclusive, role to "public authorities" (cf. Nos. 23, 33*)*.

In our own day, the state finds itself having to address the limitations to its sovereignty imposed by the new context of international trade and finance, which is characterized by increasing mobility both of financial capital and means of production, material and immaterial. This new context has altered the political power of states.

Today, as we take to heart the lessons of the current economic crisis, which sees the state's *public authorities* directly involved in correcting errors and malfunctions, it seems more realistic to *re-evaluate their role* and their powers, which need to be prudently reviewed and remodeled so as to enable them, perhaps through new forms of engagement, to address the challenges of today's world. Once the role of public authorities has been more clearly defined, one could foresee an increase in the new forms of political participation, nationally and internationally, that have come about through the activity of organizations operating in civil society; in this way it is to be hoped that the citizens' interest and participation in the *res publica* will become more deeply rooted....

27. Life in many poor countries is still extremely insecure as a consequence of food shortages, and the situation could become worse: *hunger* still reaps enormous numbers of victims among those who, like Lazarus, are not permitted to take their place at the rich man's table, contrary to the hopes expressed by Paul VI (cf. Encyclical Letter *Populorum Progressio*, No. 47). *Feed the hungry* (cf. Mt 25:35,37,42) is an ethical imperative for the universal Church, as she responds to the teachings of her Founder, the Lord Jesus, concerning solidarity and the sharing of goods. Moreover, the elimination of world hunger has also, in the global era, become a requirement for safeguarding the peace and stability of the planet. Hunger is not so much dependent on lack of material things as on shortage of social resources, the most important of which are institutional.

What is missing, in other words, is a network of economic institutions capable of guaranteeing regular access to sufficient food and water for nutritional needs, and also capable of addressing the primary needs and necessities ensuing from genuine food crises, whether due to natural causes or political irresponsibility, nationally and internationally. The problem of food insecurity needs to be addressed within a long-term perspective, eliminating the structural causes that give rise to it and promoting the agricultural development of poorer countries. This can be done by investing in rural infrastructures, irrigation systems, transport, organization of markets, and in the development and dissemination of agricultural technology that can make the best use of the human, natural, and socioeconomic resources that are more readily available at the local level, while guaranteeing their sustainability over the long term as well. All this needs to be accomplished with the involvement of local communities in choices and decisions that affect the use of agricultural land. In this perspective, it could be useful to consider the new possibilities that are opening up through proper use of traditional as well as innovative farming techniques, always assuming that these have been judged, after sufficient testing, to be appropriate, respectful of the environment, and attentive to the needs of the most deprived peoples. At the same time, the question of equitable agrarian reform in developing countries should not be ignored.

The right to food, like the right to water, has an important place within the pursuit of other rights, beginning with the fundamental right to life. It is therefore necessary to cultivate a public conscience that considers *food and access to water as universal rights of all human beings, without distinction or discrimination* (cf. Benedict XVI, *Message for the 2007 World Food Day*). It is important, moreover, to emphasize that solidarity with poor countries in the process of development can point toward a solution of the current global crisis, as politicians and directors of international institutions have begun to sense in recent times. Through support for economically poor countries by means of financial plans inspired by solidarity — so that these countries can take steps to satisfy their own citizens' demand for consumer goods and for development — not only can true economic growth be generated, but a contribution can be made toward sustaining the productive capacities of rich countries that risk being compromised by the crisis....

28. ... Openness to life is at the center of true development. When a society moves toward the denial or suppression of life, it ends up no longer finding the necessary motivation and energy to strive for man's true good. If personal and social sensitivity toward the acceptance of a new life is lost, then other forms

of acceptance that are valuable for society also wither away (cf. Benedict XVI, *Message for the 2007 World Day of Peace*, No. 5). The acceptance of life strengthens moral fiber and makes people capable of mutual help. By cultivating openness to life, wealthy peoples can better understand the needs of poor ones, they can avoid employing huge economic and intellectual resources to satisfy the selfish desires of their own citizens, and instead they can promote virtuous action within the perspective of production that is morally sound and marked by solidarity, respecting the fundamental right to life of every people and every individual....

32. ... Economic science tells us that structural insecurity generates anti-productive attitudes wasteful of human resources, inasmuch as workers tend to adapt passively to automatic mechanisms, rather than to release creativity. On this point too, there is a convergence between economic science and moral evaluation. Human costs always include economic costs, and economic dysfunctions always involve human costs.

It should be remembered that the reduction of cultures to the technological dimension, even if it favors short-term profits, in the long term impedes reciprocal enrichment and the dynamics of cooperation. It is important to distinguish between short- and long-term economic or sociological considerations. Lowering the level of protection accorded to the rights of workers, or abandoning mechanisms of wealth redistribution in order to increase the country's international competitiveness, hinder the achievement of lasting development. Moreover, the human consequences of current tendencies towards a short-term economy — sometimes very short-term — need to be carefully evaluated. This requires *further and deeper reflection on the meaning of the economy and its goals* (cf. John Paul II, *Message for the 2000 World Day of Peace*, No. 15), as well as a profound and farsighted revision of the current model of development, so as to correct its dysfunctions and deviations. This is demanded, in any case, by the earth's state of ecological health; above all it is required by the cultural and moral crisis of man, the symptoms of which have been evident for some time all over the world....

37. The Church's social doctrine has always maintained that *justice must be applied to every phase of economic activity*, because this is always concerned with man and his needs. Locating resources, financing, production, consumption, and all the other phases in the economic cycle inevitably have moral implications. *Thus every economic decision has a moral consequence.* The social sciences and the direction taken by the contemporary economy point to the same conclusion.

Perhaps at one time it was conceivable that first the creation of wealth could be entrusted to the economy, and then the task of distributing it could be assigned to politics. Today that would be more difficult, given that economic activity is no longer circumscribed within territorial limits, while the authority of governments continues to be principally local. Hence the canons of justice must be respected from the outset, as the economic process unfolds, and not just afterward or incidentally. Space also needs to be created within the market for economic activity carried out by subjects who freely choose to act according to principles other than those of pure profit, without sacrificing the production of economic value in the process. The many economic entities that draw their origin from religious and lay initiatives demonstrate that this is concretely possible.

In the global era, the economy is influenced by competitive models tied to cultures that differ greatly among themselves. The different forms of economic enterprise to which they give rise find their main point of encounter in commutative justice.

Economic life undoubtedly requires *contracts*, in order to regulate relations of exchange between goods of equivalent value. But it also needs *just laws* and *forms of redistribution* governed by politics, and what is more, it needs works redolent of the *spirit of gift*. The economy in the global era seems to privilege the former logic, that of contractual exchange, but directly or indirectly it also demonstrates its need for the other two: political logic, and the logic of the unconditional gift....

43. "The reality of human solidarity, which is a benefit for us, also imposes a duty" (Paul VI, *Populorum Progressio*, No. 17). Many people today would claim that they owe nothing to anyone, except to themselves. They are concerned only with their rights, and they often have great difficulty in taking responsibility for their own and other people's integral development. Hence it is important to call for a renewed reflection on how rights presuppose duties, if they are not to become mere license (cf. John Paul II, *Message for the 2003 World Day of Peace*, No. 5).

Nowadays we are witnessing a grave inconsistency. On the one hand, appeals are made to alleged rights, arbitrary and nonessential in nature, accompanied by the demand that they be recognized and promoted by public structures, while, on the other hand, elementary and basic rights remain unacknowledged and are violated in much of the world (cf. John Paul II, *Message for the 2003 World Day of Peace*, No. 5). A link has often been noted between claims to a "right to excess," and even to transgression and vice, within affluent societies, and the lack of food, drinkable water, basic instruction, and elementary health care in areas of the underdeveloped world and on the outskirts of large metropolitan centers. The link consists in this: individual rights, when detached from a framework of duties which grants them their full meaning, can run wild, leading to an escalation of demands which is effectively unlimited and indiscriminate.

An overemphasis on rights leads to a disregard for duties. Duties set a limit on rights because they point to the anthropological and ethical framework of which rights are a part, in this way ensuring that they do not become license. Duties thereby reinforce rights and call for their defense and promotion as a task to be undertaken in the service of the common good. Otherwise, if the only basis of human rights is to be found in the deliberations of an assembly of citizens, those rights can be changed at any time, and so the duty to respect and pursue them fades from the common consciousness. Governments and international bodies can then lose sight of the objectivity and "inviolability" of rights. When this happens, the authentic development of peoples is endangered (cf. Benedict XVI, *Message for the 2007 World Day of Peace*, No. 13). Such a way of thinking and acting compromises the authority of international bodies, especially in the eyes of those countries most in need of development. Indeed, the latter demand that the international community take up the duty of helping them to be "artisans of their own destiny" (Paul VI, *Populorum Progressio*, No. 65), that is, to take up duties of their own. *The sharing of reciprocal duties is a more powerful incentive to action than the mere assertion of rights....*

48. Today the subject of development is also closely related to the duties arising from *our relationship to the natural environment*. The environment is God's gift to everyone, and in our use of it we have a responsibility toward the poor, toward future generations, and toward humanity as a whole. When nature, including the human being, is viewed as the result of mere chance or evolutionary determinism, our sense of responsibility wanes. In nature, the believer recognizes the wonderful result of God's cre-

ative activity, which we may use responsibly to satisfy our legitimate needs, material or otherwise, while respecting the intrinsic balance of creation. If this vision is lost, we end up either considering nature an untouchable taboo or, on the contrary, abusing it. Neither attitude is consonant with the Christian vision of nature as the fruit of God's creation.

Nature expresses a design of love and truth. It is prior to us, and it has been given to us by God as the setting for our life. Nature speaks to us of the Creator (cf. Rom 1:20) and his love for humanity. It is destined to be "recapitulated" in Christ at the end of time (cf. Eph 1:9-10; Col 1:19-20). Thus it too is a "vocation" (John Paul II, *Message for the 1990 World Day of Peace*, No. 6). Nature is at our disposal not as "a heap of scattered refuse" (Heraclitus of Ephesus), but as a gift of the Creator who has given it an inbuilt order, enabling man to draw from it the principles needed in order "to till it and keep it" (Gn 2:15). But it should also be stressed that it is contrary to authentic development to view nature as something more important than the human person. This position leads to attitudes of neo-paganism or a new pantheism — human salvation cannot come from nature alone, understood in a purely naturalistic sense. This having been said, it is also necessary to reject the opposite position, which aims at total technical dominion over nature, because the natural environment is more than raw material to be manipulated at our pleasure; it is a wondrous work of the Creator containing a "grammar" which sets forth ends and criteria for its wise use, not its reckless exploitation.

Today much harm is done to development precisely as a result of these distorted notions. Reducing nature merely to a collection of contingent data ends up doing violence to the environment and even encouraging activity that fails to respect human nature itself. Our nature, constituted not only by matter but also by spirit, and as such endowed with transcendent meaning and aspirations, is also normative for culture. Human beings interpret and shape the natural environment through culture, which in turn is given direction by the responsible use of freedom, in accordance with the dictates of the moral law. Consequently, projects for integral human development cannot ignore coming generations, but need to be *marked by solidarity and inter-generational justice*, while taking into account a variety of contexts: ecological, juridical, economic, political, and cultural (*Compendium of the Social Doctrine of the Church*, Nos. 451-487).

49. Questions linked to the care and preservation of the environment today need to give due consideration to *the energy problem*. The fact that some states, power groups and companies hoard nonrenewable energy resources represents a grave obstacle to development in poor countries. Those countries lack the economic means either to gain access to existing sources of nonrenewable energy or to finance research into new alternatives. The stockpiling of natural resources, which in many cases are found in the poor countries themselves, gives rise to exploitation and frequent conflicts between and within nations. These conflicts are often fought on the soil of those same countries, with a heavy toll of death, destruction, and further decay. The international community has an urgent duty to find institutional means of regulating the exploitation of nonrenewable resources, involving poor countries in the process, in order to plan together for the future.

On this front too, there is a *pressing moral need for renewed solidarity*, especially in relationships between developing countries and those that are highly industrialized (cf. John Paul II,

Message for the 1990 World Day of Peace, No. 10). The technologically advanced societies can and must lower their domestic energy consumption, either through an evolution in manufacturing methods or through greater ecological sensitivity among their citizens. It should be added that at present it is possible to achieve improved energy efficiency while at the same time encouraging research into alternative forms of energy. What is also needed, though, is a worldwide redistribution of energy resources, so that countries lacking those resources can have access to them. The fate of those countries cannot be left in the hands of whoever is first to claim the spoils, or whoever is able to prevail over the rest. Here we are dealing with major issues; if they are to be faced adequately, then everyone must responsibly recognize the impact they will have on future generations, particularly on the many young people in the poorer nations, who "ask to assume their active part in the construction of a better world" (Paul VI, *Populorum Progressio*, No. 65).

50. This responsibility is a global one, for it is concerned not just with energy but with the whole of creation, which must not be bequeathed to future generations depleted of its resources. Human beings legitimately exercise a *responsible stewardship over nature*, in order to protect it, to enjoy its fruits and to cultivate it in new ways, with the assistance of advanced technologies, so that it can worthily accommodate and feed the world's population. On this earth there is room for everyone: here the entire human family must find the resources to live with dignity, through the help of nature itself — God's gift to his children — and through hard work and creativity. At the same time we must recognize our grave duty to hand the earth on to future generations in such a condition that they too can worthily inhabit it and continue to cultivate it. This means being committed to

making joint decisions "after pondering responsibly the road to be taken, decisions aimed at strengthening that *covenant between human beings and the environment*, which should mirror the creative love of God, from whom we come and toward whom we are journeying" (Benedict XVI, *Message for the 2008 World Day of Peace*, No. 7).

Let us hope that the international community and individual governments will succeed in countering harmful ways of treating the environment. It is likewise incumbent upon the competent authorities to make every effort to ensure that the economic and social costs of using up shared environmental resources are recognized with transparency and fully borne by those who incur them, not by other peoples or future generations: the protection of the environment, of resources, and of the climate obliges all international leaders to act jointly and to show a readiness to work in good faith, respecting the law and promoting solidarity with the weakest regions of the planet (cf. Benedict XVI, *Address to the General Assembly of the United Nations Organization*, New York, April 18, 2008). One of the greatest challenges facing the economy is to achieve the most efficient use — not abuse — of natural resources, based on a realization that the notion of "efficiency" is not value-free.

51. *The way humanity treats the environment influences the way it treats itself, and vice versa.* This invites contemporary society to a serious review of its lifestyle, which, in many parts of the world, is prone to hedonism and consumerism, regardless of their harmful consequences (cf. John Paul II, *Message for the 1990 World Day of Peace*, No. 13). What is needed is an effective shift in mentality which can lead to the adoption of *new lifestyles* "in which the quest for truth, beauty, goodness, and communion with others for the sake of common growth are the factors which

determine consumer choices, savings, and investments" (John Paul II, *Centesimus Annus*, No. 36). Every violation of solidarity and civic friendship harms the environment, just as environmental deterioration in turn upsets relations in society.

Nature, especially in our time, is so integrated into the dynamics of society and culture that by now it hardly constitutes an independent variable. Desertification and the decline in productivity in some agricultural areas are also the result of impoverishment and underdevelopment among their inhabitants. When incentives are offered for their economic and cultural development, nature itself is protected. Moreover, how many natural resources are squandered by wars! Peace in and among peoples would also provide greater protection for nature. The hoarding of resources, especially water, can generate serious conflicts among the peoples involved. Peaceful agreement about the use of resources can protect nature and, at the same time, the well-being of the societies concerned.

The Church has a responsibility toward creation, and she must assert this responsibility in the public sphere. In so doing, she must defend not only earth, water, and air as gifts of creation that belong to everyone. She must above all protect mankind from self-destruction. There is need for what might be called a human ecology, correctly understood. The deterioration of nature is in fact closely connected to the culture that shapes human coexistence: *when "human ecology" (Ibid., No. 38) is respected within society, environmental ecology also benefits.* Just as human virtues are interrelated, such that the weakening of one places others at risk, so the ecological system is based on respect for a plan that affects both the health of society and its good relationship with nature.

In order to protect nature, it is not enough to intervene with economic incentives or deterrents; not even an apposite education is sufficient. These are important steps, but *the decisive issue is the overall moral tenor of society*. If there is a lack of respect for the right to life and to a natural death, if human conception, gestation, and birth are made artificial, if human embryos are sacrificed to research, the conscience of society ends up losing the concept of human ecology and, along with it, that of environmental ecology. It is contradictory to insist that future generations respect the natural environment when our educational systems and laws do not help them to respect themselves. The book of nature is one and indivisible: it takes in not only the environment, but also life, sexuality, marriage, the family, social relations: in a word, integral human development. Our duties toward the environment are linked to our duties toward the human person, considered in himself and in relation to others. It would be wrong to uphold one set of duties while trampling on the other. Herein lies a grave contradiction in our mentality and practice today: one which demeans the person, disrupts the environment, and damages society.

52. Truth, and the love which it reveals, cannot be produced: they can only be received as a gift. Their ultimate source is not, and cannot be, mankind, but only God, who is himself Truth and Love. This principle is extremely important for society and for development, since neither can be a purely human product; the vocation to development on the part of individuals and peoples is not based simply on human choice, but is an intrinsic part of a plan that is prior to us and constitutes for all of us a duty to be freely accepted. That which is prior to us and constitutes us — subsistent Love and Truth — shows us what goodness is, and in what our true happiness consists. *It shows us the road to true development.* ...

61. Greater solidarity at the international level is seen especially in the ongoing promotion — even in the midst of economic crisis — of *greater access to education*, which is at the same time an essential precondition for effective international cooperation. The term "education" refers not only to classroom teaching and vocational training — both of which are important factors in development — but to the complete formation of the person. In this regard, there is a problem that should be highlighted: in order to educate, it is necessary to know the nature of the human person, to know who he or she is. The increasing prominence of a relativistic understanding of that nature presents serious problems for education, especially moral education, jeopardizing its universal extension. Yielding to this kind of relativism makes everyone poorer and has a negative impact on the effectiveness of aid to the most needy populations, who lack not only economic and technical means, but also educational methods and resources to assist people in realizing their full human potential.

An illustration of the significance of this problem is offered by the phenomenon of *international tourism* (cf. Benedict XVI, *Address to the Bishops of Thailand on their "Ad Limina" Visit*, May 16, 2008), which can be a major factor in economic development and cultural growth, but can also become an occasion for exploitation and moral degradation. The current situation offers unique opportunities for the economic aspects of development — that is to say the flow of money and the emergence of a significant amount of local enterprise — to be combined with the cultural aspects, chief among which is education. In many cases this is what happens, but in other cases international tourism has a negative educational impact both for the tourist and the local populace. The latter are often exposed to immoral or even perverted forms of conduct, as in the case of so-called sex tourism, to which many human beings are sacrificed even at a tender age. It is sad to note that this activity often takes place with the support of local governments, with silence from those in the tourists' countries of origin, and with the complicity of many of the tour operators. Even in less extreme cases, international tourism often follows a consumerist and hedonistic pattern, as a form of escapism planned in a manner typical of the countries of origin, and therefore not conducive to authentic encounter between persons and cultures. We need, therefore, to develop a different type of tourism that has the ability to promote genuine mutual understanding, without taking away from the element of rest and healthy recreation. Tourism of this type needs to increase, partly through closer coordination with the experience gained from international cooperation and enterprise for development....

70. Technological development can give rise to the idea that technology is self-sufficient when too much attention is given to the "*how*" questions, and not enough to the many "*why*" questions underlying human activity. For this reason technology can appear ambivalent. Produced through human creativity as a tool of personal freedom, technology can be understood as a manifestation of absolute freedom, the freedom that seeks to prescind from the limits inherent in things. The process of globalization could replace ideologies with technology (cf. Paul VI, *Octogesima Adveniens,* No. 29), allowing the latter to become an ideological power that threatens to confine us within an *a priori* that holds us back from encountering being and truth. Were that to happen, we would all know, evaluate, and make decisions about our life situations from within a technocratic cultural perspective to which we would belong structurally, without ever being able to discover a meaning that is not of our own making. The "technical" worldview that follows from this vision is now so dominant

that truth has come to be seen as coinciding with the possible. But when the sole criterion of truth is efficiency and utility, development is automatically denied. True development does not consist primarily in "doing."

The key to development is a mind capable of thinking in technological terms and grasping the fully human meaning of human activities, within the context of the holistic meaning of the individual's being. Even when we work through satellites or through remote electronic impulses, our actions always remain human, an expression of our responsible freedom. Technology is highly attractive because it draws us out of our physical limitations and broadens our horizon. *But human freedom is authentic only when it responds to the fascination of technology with decisions that are the fruit of moral responsibility.* Hence the pressing need for formation in an ethically responsible use of technology. Moving beyond the fascination that technology exerts, we must reappropriate the true meaning of freedom, which is not an intoxication with total autonomy, but a response to the call of being, beginning with our own personal being.

Precious Gift of Creation[30]

We have almost reached the end of August, which for many means the end of the summer holidays. As we pick up our usual routine, how could we not thank God for the precious gift of creation which we so enjoy, and not only during our holidays! The various phenomena of environmental degradation and natural disasters which, unfortunately, are often reported in the news remind us of the urgent need to respect nature as we should, recovering and appreciating a correct relationship with the environment in everyday life. A new sensitivity to these topics that justly give rise to concern on the part of the authorities and of public opinion is developing and is expressed in the increasing number of meetings, also at the international level.

The Earth is indeed a precious gift of the Creator who, in designing its intrinsic order, has given us bearings that guide us as stewards of his creation. Precisely from within this framework, the Church considers matters concerning the environment and its protection intimately linked to the theme of integral human development. In my Encyclical *Caritas in Veritate,* I referred more than once to such questions, recalling the "pressing moral need for renewed solidarity" (No.. 49) not only between countries but also between individuals, since the natural environment is given by God to everyone, and our use of it entails a personal responsibility toward humanity as a whole, and in particular toward the poor and towards future generations (cf. No. 48).

Bearing in mind our common responsibility for creation (cf. No. 51), the Church is not only committed to promoting the protection of land, water, and air as gifts of the Creator destined to everyone, but above all she invites others and works herself to protect mankind from self-destruction. In fact, "when 'human

---

30 Pope Benedict XVI, General Audience, August 26, 2009.

ecology' is respected within society, environmental ecology also benefits" (*ibid.*). Is it not true that an irresponsible use of creation begins precisely where God is marginalized or even denied? If the relationship between human creatures and the Creator is forgotten, matter is reduced to a selfish possession, man becomes the "last word," and the purpose of human existence is reduced to a scramble for the maximum number of possessions possible.

The created world, structured in an intelligent way by God, is entrusted to our responsibility, and though we are able to analyze it and transform it we cannot consider ourselves creation's absolute master. We are called, rather, to exercise responsible stewardship of creation, in order to protect it, to enjoy its fruits, and to cultivate it, finding the resources necessary for everyone to live with dignity. Through the help of nature itself and through hard work and creativity, humanity is indeed capable of carrying out its grave duty to hand on the earth to future generations so that they too, in turn, will be able to inhabit it worthily and continue to cultivate it (cf. No. 50). For this to happen, it is essential to develop "that covenant between human beings and the environment, which should mirror the creative love of God" (*Message for the 2008 World Day of Peace,* No. 7), recognizing that we all come from God and that we are all journeying toward him. How important it is then, that the international community and individual governments send the right signals to their citizens to succeed in countering harmful ways of treating the environment!

The economic and social costs of using up shared environmental resources must be recognized with transparency and borne by those who incur them, and not by other peoples or future generations. The protection of the environment, and the safeguarding of resources and of the climate, oblige all international leaders to act jointly, respecting the law and promoting solidarity with the weakest regions of the world (cf. *Caritas in Veritate,* No. 50). Together we can build an integral human development beneficial for all peoples, present and future, a development inspired by the values of charity in truth. For this to happen it is essential that the current model of global development be transformed through a greater, and shared, acceptance of responsibility for creation: this is demanded not only by environmental factors, but also by the scandal of hunger and human misery.

Dear brothers and sisters, let us now give thanks to the Lord and make our own the words of Saint Francis found in "The Canticle of All Creatures":

"Most High, all-powerful, all-good Lord,

"All praise is Yours, all glory, all honor and all blessings.

"To you alone, Most High, do they belong...."

So says Saint Francis. We, too, wish to pray and live in the spirit of these words.

The theme chosen by the Food and Agriculture Organization (FAO) for World Food Day is: *"Achieving food security in times of crisis."* It is an invitation to consider agricultural work as a fundamental element of food security and consequently as fully part of economic activity. For this reason, farming must have access to adequate investments and resources. This topic calls into question and makes clear that by their nature the goods of creation are limited: they therefore require responsible attitudes capable of encouraging the sought-after security, thinking likewise of that of future generations. Thus profound solidarity and farsighted brotherhood are essential.

The realization of these objectives entails a necessary change in lifestyle and mind-sets. It obliges the international community and its institutions to intervene in a more appropriate and forceful way. I hope that such an intervention may encourage cooperation with a view to protecting the methods of cultivating the land proper to each region and to avoiding a heedless use of natural resources. I also hope that this cooperation will preserve the values proper to the rural world and the fundamental rights of those who work the land. By setting aside privileges, profit, and convenience, it will then be possible to achieve these objectives for the benefit of the men, women, children, families, and communities that live in the poorest regions of the planet and are the most vulnerable. Experience shows that even advanced technical solutions lack efficiency if they do not put the person first and foremost, who comes first and who, in his or her spiritual and physical dimensions, is the alpha and the omega of all activity.

---

31 Pope Benedict XVI, Message to the Director General of the Food and Agriculture Organization, October 16, 2009.

Rather than an elementary need, access to food is a fundamental right of people and peoples. It will therefore become a reality, hence a security, if adequate development is guaranteed in all the different regions. The drama of hunger in particular can only be overcome by "eliminating the structural causes that give rise to it and promoting the agricultural development of the poorer countries. This can be done by investing in rural infrastructures, irrigation systems, transport, organization of markets, and in the development and dissemination of appropriate agricultural technology that can make the best use of the human, natural, and socioeconomic resources that are more readily available at the local level" (*Caritas in Veritate,* No. 27).

Faithful to her vocation to be close to the most deprived, the Catholic Church promotes, sustains, and participates in the efforts made to enable each people and each community to have access to the necessary means to guarantee an appropriate level of food security.

In expressing these wishes, I renew to you, Mr. Director-General, the expression of my high esteem, and I invoke an abundance of divine blessings upon the FAO, upon the member states, and upon all the personnel.

8. Methods of food production likewise demand attentive analysis of the relationship between development and *protection of the environment*. The desire to possess and to exploit the resources of the planet in an excessive and disordered manner is the primary cause of all environmental degradation. Protection of the environment challenges the modern world to guarantee a harmonious form of development, respectful of the design of God the creator, and therefore capable of safeguarding the planet (cf. *Caritas in Veritate*, Nos. 48-51). While the entire human race is called to acknowledge its obligations to future generations, it is also true that states and international organizations have a duty to protect the environment as a shared good. In this context, the links between environmental security and the disturbing phenomenon of climate change need to be explored further, focusing on the central importance of the human person, and especially of the populations most at risk from both phenomena. Norms, legislation, development plans, and investments are not enough, however: what is needed is a change in the lifestyles of individuals and communities, in habits of consumption, and in perceptions of what is genuinely needed. Most of all, there is a moral duty to distinguish between good and evil in human action, so as to rediscover the bond of communion that unites the human person and creation.

9. As I pointed out in the Encyclical Letter *Caritas in Veritate*, it is important to remember that "the deterioration of nature is ... closely connected to the culture that shapes human coexistence: *when 'human ecology' is respected within society, environmental ecology also benefits*." Indeed, "the ecological system is based on respect for a plan that affects both the health of society

---

32 Pope Benedict XVI, Address to FAO on Occasion of the World Summit on Food Security, November 16, 2009.

and its good relationship with nature." And "*the decisive issue is the overall moral tenor of society.*" Therefore, "our duties toward the environment are linked to our duties toward the human person, considered in himself and in relation to others. It would be wrong to uphold one set of duties while trampling on the other. Herein lies a grave contradiction in our mentality and practice today: one which demeans the person, disrupts the environment and damages society" (*ibid.*, No. 51).

1. At the beginning of this New Year, I wish to offer heartfelt greetings of peace to all Christian communities, international leaders, and people of good will throughout the world. For this XLIII World Day of Peace I have chosen the theme: *If You Want to Cultivate Peace, Protect Creation*. Respect for creation is of immense consequence, not least because "creation is the beginning and the foundation of all God's works" (*Catechism of the Catholic Church*, No. 198), and its preservation has now become essential for the pacific coexistence of mankind. Man's inhumanity to man has given rise to numerous threats to peace and to authentic and integral human development — wars, international and regional conflicts, acts of terrorism, and violations of human rights. Yet no less troubling are the threats arising from the neglect — if not downright misuse — of the earth and the natural goods that God has given us. For this reason, it is imperative that mankind renew and strengthen "that covenant between human beings and the environment, which should mirror the creative love of God, from whom we come and toward whom we are journeying" (*Message for the World Day of Peace*, 2008).

2. In my Encyclical *Caritas in Veritate*, I noted that integral human development is closely linked to the obligations which flow from *man's relationship with the natural environment*. The environment must be seen as God's gift to all people, and the use we make of it entails a shared responsibility for all humanity, especially the poor and future generations. I also observed that whenever nature, and human beings in particular, are seen merely as products of chance or an evolutionary determinism, our overall sense of responsibility wanes (cf. No. 48). On the other hand, seeing creation as God's gift to humanity helps us

---

33 Pope Benedict XVI, Message for the Celebration of the World Day of Peace, January 1, 2010.

understand our vocation and worth as human beings. With the Psalmist, we can exclaim with wonder: "When I look at your heavens, the work of your hands, the moon and the stars which you have established; what is man that you are mindful of him, and the son of man that you care for him?" (Ps 8:4-5). Contemplating the beauty of creation inspires us to recognize the love of the Creator, that Love which "moves the sun and the other stars" (Dante Alighieri, *The Divine Comedy, Paradiso*, XXXIII, 145).

3. Twenty years ago, Pope John Paul II devoted his *Message for the World Day of Peace* to the theme: *Peace with God the Creator, Peace with All of Creation*. He emphasized our relationship, as God's creatures, with the universe all around us. "In our day," he wrote, "there is a growing awareness that world peace is threatened … also by a lack of *due respect for nature.*" He added that "*ecological awareness,* rather than being downplayed, needs to be helped to develop and mature, and find fitting expression in concrete programs and initiatives" (*Message for the 1990 World Day of Peace*). Previous popes had spoken of the relationship between human beings and the environment. In 1971, for example, on the eightieth anniversary of Leo XIII's Encyclical *Rerum Novarum*, Paul VI pointed out that "by an ill-considered exploitation of nature (man) risks destroying it and becoming in his turn the victim of this degradation." He added that "not only is the material environment becoming a permanent menace — pollution and refuse, new illnesses and absolute destructive capacity — but the human framework is no longer under man's control, thus creating an environment for tomorrow which may well be intolerable. This is a wide-ranging social problem which concerns the entire human family" (*Octogesima Adveniens*, No. 21).

4. Without entering into the merit of specific technical solutions, the Church is nonetheless concerned, as an "expert in

humanity," to call attention to the relationship between the Creator, human beings, and the created order. In 1990, John Paul II had spoken of an "ecological crisis" and, in highlighting its primarily ethical character, pointed to the "urgent moral need for a new solidarity" (*Message for the 1990 World Day of Peace*). His appeal is all the more pressing today, in the face of signs of a growing crisis which it would be irresponsible not to take seriously. Can we remain indifferent before the problems associated with such realities as climate change, desertification, the deterioration and loss of productivity in vast agricultural areas, the pollution of rivers and aquifers, the loss of biodiversity, the increase of natural catastrophes, and the deforestation of equatorial and tropical regions? Can we disregard the growing phenomenon of "environmental refugees," people who are forced by the degradation of their natural habitat to forsake it — and often their possessions as well — in order to face the dangers and uncertainties of forced displacement? Can we remain impassive in the face of actual and potential conflicts involving access to natural resources? All these are issues with a profound impact on the exercise of human rights, such as the right to life, food, health, and development.

5. It should be evident that the ecological crisis cannot be viewed in isolation from other related questions, since it is closely linked to the notion of development itself and our understanding of man in his relationship to others and to the rest of creation. Prudence would thus dictate a *profound, long-term review of our model of development,* one which would take into consideration the meaning of the economy and its goals with an eye to correcting its malfunctions and misapplications. The ecological health of the planet calls for this, but it is also demanded by the cultural and moral crisis of humanity whose symptoms

have for some time been evident in every part of the world (cf. *Caritas in Veritate*, No. 32). Humanity needs a *profound cultural renewal;* it needs to *rediscover those values which can serve as the solid basis* for building a brighter future for all. Our present crises — be they economic, food-related, environmental, or social — are ultimately also moral crises, and all of them are interrelated. They require us to rethink the path which we are traveling together. Specifically, they call for a lifestyle marked by sobriety and solidarity, with new rules and forms of engagement, one which focuses confidently and courageously on strategies that actually work, while decisively rejecting those that have failed. Only in this way can the current crisis become an *opportunity for discernment and new strategic planning.*

6. Is it not true that what we call "nature" in a cosmic sense has its origin in "a plan of love and truth"? The world "is not the product of any necessity whatsoever, nor of blind fate or chance.... The world proceeds from the free will of God; he wanted to make his creatures share in his being, in his intelligence, and in his goodness" (*Catechism of the Catholic Church*, No. 295). The *Book of Genesis*, in its very first pages, points to the wise design of the cosmos: it comes forth from God's mind and finds its culmination in man and woman, made in the image and likeness of the Creator to "fill the earth" and to "have dominion over" it as "stewards" of God himself (cf. Gn 1:28). The harmony between the Creator, mankind, and the created world, as described by Sacred Scripture, was disrupted by the sin of Adam and Eve, by man and woman, who wanted to take the place of God and refused to acknowledge that they were his creatures. As a result, the work of "exercising dominion" over the earth, "tilling it and keeping it," was also disrupted, and conflict arose within and between mankind and the rest of creation (cf. Gn 3:17-19).

TO CULTIVATE PEACE, PROTECT CREATION

Human beings let themselves be mastered by selfishness; they misunderstood the meaning of God's command and exploited creation out of a desire to exercise absolute domination over it. But the true meaning of God's original command, as the *Book of Genesis* clearly shows, was not a simple conferral of authority, but rather a summons to responsibility.

The wisdom of the ancients had recognized that nature is not at our disposal as "a heap of scattered refuse" (Heraclitus of Ephesus). Biblical revelation made us see that nature is a gift of the Creator, who gave it an inbuilt order and enabled man to draw from it the principles needed to "till it and keep it" (cf. Gn 2:15) (cf. *Caritas in Veritate*, No. 48). Everything that exists belongs to God, who has entrusted it to man, albeit not for his arbitrary use. Once man, instead of acting as God's co-worker, sets himself up in place of God, he ends up provoking a rebellion on the part of nature, "which is more tyrannized than governed by him" (John Paul II, *Centesimus Annus*, No. 37). Man thus has a duty to exercise responsible stewardship over creation, to care for it and to cultivate it (cf. *Caritas in Veritate*, No. 50).

7. Sad to say, it is all too evident that large numbers of people in different countries and areas of our planet are experiencing increased hardship because of the negligence or refusal of many others to exercise responsible stewardship over the environment. The Second Vatican Council reminded us that "God has destined the earth and everything it contains for all peoples and nations" (*Gaudium et Spes*, No. 69). The goods of creation belong to humanity as a whole. Yet the current pace of environmental exploitation is seriously endangering the supply of certain natural resources not only for the present generation, but above all for generations yet to come (cf. John Paul II, *Sollicitudo Rei Socialis*, No. 34). It is not hard to see that environmental degradation

is often due to the lack of farsighted official policies or to the pursuit of myopic economic interests, which then, tragically, become a serious threat to creation. To combat this phenomenon, economic activity needs to consider the fact that "every economic decision has a moral consequence" (*Caritas in Veritate*, No. 37) and thus show increased respect for the environment.

When making use of natural resources, we should be concerned for their protection and consider the cost entailed — environmentally and socially — as an essential part of the overall expenses incurred. The international community and national governments are responsible for sending the right signals in order to combat effectively the misuse of the environment. To protect the environment, and to safeguard natural resources and the climate, there is a need to act in accordance with clearly defined rules, also from the juridical and economic standpoint, while at the same time taking into due account the solidarity we owe to those living in the poorer areas of our world and to future generations.

8. *A greater sense of intergenerational solidarity* is urgently needed. Future generations cannot be saddled with the cost of our use of common environmental resources. "We have inherited from past generations, and we have benefited from the work of our contemporaries; for this reason we have obligations toward all, and we cannot refuse to interest ourselves in those who will come after us, to enlarge the human family. Universal solidarity represents a benefit as well as a duty. *This is a responsibility that present generations have toward those of the future*, a responsibility that also concerns individual states and the international community" (*Compendium of the Social Doctrine of the Church*, No. 467).

Natural resources should be used in such a way that immediate benefits do not have a negative impact on living creatures, human and not, present and future; that the protection of private property does not conflict with the universal destination of goods (cf. John Paul II, *Centesimus Annus*, Nos. 30-31, 43); that human activity does not compromise the fruitfulness of the earth, for the benefit of people now and in the future. In addition to a fairer sense of intergenerational solidarity there is also an urgent moral need for a renewed sense of *intragenerational solidarity*, especially in relationships between developing countries and highly industrialized countries: "the international community has an urgent duty to find institutional means of regulating the exploitation of nonrenewable resources, involving poor countries in the process, in order to plan together for the future" (*Caritas in Veritate*, No. 49).

The ecological crisis shows the urgency of a solidarity which embraces time and space. It is important to acknowledge that among the causes of the present ecological crisis is the historical responsibility of the industrialized countries. Yet the less developed countries, and emerging countries in particular, are not exempt from their own responsibilities with regard to creation, for the duty of gradually adopting effective environmental measures and policies is incumbent upon all. This would be accomplished more easily if self-interest played a lesser role in the granting of aid and the sharing of knowledge and cleaner technologies.

9. To be sure, among the basic problems which the international community has to address is that of energy resources and the development of joint and sustainable strategies to satisfy the energy needs of the present and future generations. This means that technologically advanced societies must be prepared to encourage more sober lifestyles, while reducing their energy con-

sumption and improving its efficiency. At the same time there is a need to encourage research into, and utilization of, forms of energy with lower impact on the environment and "a worldwide redistribution of energy resources, so that countries lacking those resources can have access to them" (*Caritas in Veritate*, No. 49).

The ecological crisis offers a historic opportunity to develop a common plan of action aimed at orienting the model of global development toward greater respect for creation and for an integral human development inspired by the values proper to charity in truth. I would advocate the adoption of a model of development based on the centrality of the human person, on the promotion and sharing of the common good, on responsibility, on a realization of our need for a changed lifestyle, and on prudence, the virtue which tells us what needs to be done today in view of what might happen tomorrow (cf. Saint Thomas Aquinas, *Summa Theologiae*, II-II, q. 49, 5).

10. A sustainable comprehensive management of the environment and the resources of the planet demands that human intelligence be directed to technological and scientific research and its practical applications. The "new solidarity" for which John Paul II called in his *Message for the 1990 World Day of Peace* (cf. No. 9) and the "global solidarity" for which I myself appealed in my *Message for the 2009 World Day of Peace* (cf. No. 8) are essential attitudes in shaping our efforts to protect creation through a better internationally coordinated management of the earth's resources, particularly today, when there is an increasingly clear link between combating environmental degradation and promoting an integral human development. These two realities are inseparable, since "the integral development of individuals necessarily entails a joint effort for the development of humanity as a whole" (Paul VI, *Populorum Progressio*, No. 43).

At present there are a number of scientific developments and innovative approaches which promise to provide satisfactory and balanced solutions to the problem of our relationship to the environment. Encouragement needs to be given, for example, to research into effective ways of exploiting the immense potential of solar energy. Similar attention also needs to be paid to the worldwide problem of water and to the global-water-cycle system, which is of prime importance for life on earth and whose stability could be seriously jeopardized by climate change. Suitable strategies for rural development centered on small farmers and their families should be explored, as well as the implementation of appropriate policies for the management of forests, for waste disposal, and for strengthening the linkage between combating climate change and overcoming poverty. Ambitious national policies are required, together with a necessary international commitment which will offer important benefits, especially in the medium and long term.

There is a need, in effect, to move beyond a purely consumerist mentality in order to promote forms of agricultural and industrial production capable of respecting creation and satisfying the primary needs of all. The ecological problem must be dealt with not only because of the chilling prospects of environmental degradation on the horizon; the real motivation must be the quest for authentic worldwide solidarity inspired by the values of charity, justice, and the common good. For that matter, as I have stated elsewhere, "technology is never merely technology. It reveals man and his aspirations toward development; it expresses the inner tension that impels him gradually to overcome material limitations. *Technology in this sense is a response to God's command to till and keep the land* (cf. Gn 2:15) that he has entrusted to humanity, and it must serve to reinforce the covenant between human beings and the environment, a covenant that should mirror God's creative love" (*Caritas in Veritate*, No. 69).

11. It is becoming more and more evident that the issue of environmental degradation challenges us to examine our lifestyle and the prevailing models of consumption and production, which are often unsustainable from a social, environmental, and even economic point of view. We can no longer do without a real change of outlook which will result in *new lifestyles*, "in which the quest for truth, beauty, goodness, and communion with others for the sake of common growth are the factors which determine consumer choices, savings, and investments" (John Paul II, *Centesimus Annus*, No. 36).

Education for peace must increasingly begin with far-reaching decisions on the part of individuals, families, communities, and states. We are all responsible for the protection and care of the environment. This responsibility knows no boundaries. In accordance with the *principle of subsidiarity* it is important for everyone to be committed at his or her proper level, working to overcome the prevalence of particular interests. A special role in raising awareness and in formation belongs to the different groups present in civil society and to the nongovernmental organizations which work with determination and generosity for the spread of ecological responsibility, responsibility which should be ever more deeply anchored in respect for "human ecology."

The media also have a responsibility in this regard to offer positive and inspiring models. In a word, concern for the environment calls for a broad global vision of the world; a responsible common effort to move beyond approaches based on selfish nationalistic interests toward a vision constantly open to the needs of all peoples. We cannot remain indifferent to what is happening around us, for the deterioration of any one part of the planet affects us all. Relationships between individuals, social groups, and states, like those between human beings and the environment, must be marked by respect and "charity in truth." In this broader context one can only encourage the efforts of the international community to ensure progressive disarmament and a world free of nuclear weapons, whose presence alone threatens the life of the planet and the ongoing integral development of the present generation and of generations yet to come.

12. *The Church has a responsibility towards creation*, and she considers it her duty to exercise that responsibility in public life, in order to protect earth, water, and air as gifts of God the Creator meant for everyone, and above all to save mankind from the danger of self-destruction. The degradation of nature is closely linked to the cultural models shaping human coexistence: consequently, "when 'human ecology' is respected within society, environmental ecology also benefits" (*Caritas in Veritate*, No. 51). Young people cannot be asked to respect the environment if they are not helped, within families and society as a whole, to respect themselves. The book of nature is one and indivisible; it includes not only the environment but also individual, family, and social ethics (cf. *ibid.*, Nos. 15, 51). Our duties toward the environment flow from our duties toward the person, considered both individually and in relation to others.

Hence I readily encourage efforts to promote a greater sense of ecological responsibility which, as I indicated in my Encyclical *Caritas in Veritate*, would safeguard an authentic "human ecology" and thus forcefully reaffirm the inviolability of human life at every stage and in every condition, the dignity of the person and the unique mission of the family, where one is trained in love of neighbor and respect for nature (cf. *ibid.*, Nos. 28, 51, 61). There is a need to safeguard the human patrimony of society.

This patrimony of values originates in and is part of the natural moral law, which is the foundation of respect for the human person and creation.

13. Nor must we forget the very significant fact that many people experience peace and tranquility, renewal and reinvigoration, when they come into close contact with the beauty and harmony of nature. There exists a certain reciprocity: as we care for creation, we realize that God, through creation, cares for us. On the other hand, a correct understanding of the relationship between man and the environment will not end by absolutizing nature or by considering it more important than the human person.

If the Church's magisterium expresses grave misgivings about notions of the environment inspired by ecocentrism and biocentrism, it is because such notions eliminate the difference of identity and worth between the human person and other living things. In the name of a supposedly egalitarian vision of the "dignity" of all living creatures, such notions end up abolishing the distinctiveness and superior role of human beings. They also open the way to a new pantheism tinged with neo-paganism, which would see the source of man's salvation in nature alone, understood in purely naturalistic terms.

The Church, for her part, is concerned that the question be approached in a balanced way, with respect for the "grammar" which the Creator has inscribed in his handiwork by giving man the role of a steward and administrator with responsibility over creation, a role which man must certainly not abuse, but also one which he may not abdicate. In the same way, the opposite position, which would absolutize technology and human power, results in a grave assault not only on nature, but also on human dignity itself (cf. *Caritas in Veritate*, No. 70).

14. *If you want to cultivate peace, protect creation.* The quest for peace by people of good will surely would become easier if all acknowledge the indivisible relationship between God, human beings, and the whole of creation. In the light of divine Revelation and in fidelity to the Church's Tradition, Christians have their own contribution to make. They contemplate the cosmos and its marvels in light of the creative work of the Father and the redemptive work of Christ, who by his death and resurrection has reconciled with God "all things, whether on earth or in heaven" (Col 1:20). Christ, crucified and risen, has bestowed his Spirit of holiness upon mankind, to guide the course of history in anticipation of that day when, with the glorious return of the Savior, there will be "new heavens and a new earth" (2 Pt 3:13), in which justice and peace will dwell for ever.

Protecting the natural environment in order to build a world of peace is thus a duty incumbent upon each and all. It is an urgent challenge, one to be faced with renewed and concerted commitment; it is also a providential opportunity to hand down to coming generations the prospect of a better future for all. May this be clear to world leaders and to those at every level who are concerned for the future of humanity: the protection of creation and peacemaking are profoundly linked! For this reason, I invite all believers to raise a fervent prayer to God, the all-powerful Creator and the Father of mercies, so that all men and women may take to heart the urgent appeal: *If you want to cultivate peace, protect creation.*

My *Message for the 43rd World Day of Peace*, "If You Want to Cultivate Peace, Protect Creation," fits within the perspective of God's Face and of human faces. Indeed, we can say that the human being is capable of respecting creatures insofar as he bears in his mind a full sense of life, otherwise he will be inclined to despise himself and all that surrounds him, to have no respect for the environment in which he lives and no respect for Creation. Those who can recognize in the cosmos the reflections of the Creator's invisible face, tend to have greater love for creatures and greater sensitivity to their symbolic value. The Book of Psalms is especially rich in testimonies of this truly human way of relating to nature: to the sky, the sea, mountains, hills, rivers, animals.... "O Lord, how manifold are your works!" the Psalmist explains. "In wisdom have you made them all; / the earth is full of your creatures" (Ps 104[103]:24).

The perspective of the "face" in particular invites us to reflect on what, also in this message, I have called "human ecology." In fact there is a very close connection between respect for the human being and the safeguard of creation. "Our duties toward the environment flow from our duties toward the person, considered both individually and in relation to others" (No. 12). If the person becomes degenerate the environment in which he lives deteriorates; if culture is inclined to nihilism ... nature cannot but pay the consequences. In fact, it is possible to note a reciprocal influence between the human face and the "face" of the environment: "when 'human ecology' is respected within society, environmental ecology also benefits" (*Caritas in Veritate*, No. 51). I therefore renew my appeal to invest in education, proposing as an objective, in addition to the necessary transmission

---

34 Pope Benedict XVI, Homily, January 1, 2010.

of technical and scientific notions, a broader and deeper "eco-logical responsibility," based on respect for human beings and their fundamental rights and duties. Only in this way can the commitment to the environment truly become an education in peace and in building peace.

Dear brothers and sisters, a psalm recurs in the Christmas season that contains, amongst other things, a wonderful example of how God's coming will transfigure the creation and give rise to a sort of cosmic celebration. This hymn begins with an invitation to all peoples to praise: "Sing to the Lord a new song; / sing to the Lord, all the earth! / Sing to the Lord, bless his Name" (Ps 96[95]:1). Yet at a certain point this appeal for exultation is extended to the whole of creation: "Let the Heavens be glad, and let the earth rejoice; / let the sea roar, and all that fills it; / let the field exalt, and everything in it! / Then shall all the trees of the wood sing for joy" (vv. 11-12). The celebration of faith becomes a celebration of the human being and of creation: that celebration which is also expressed at Christmas in decorations on trees, in streets, and in houses. Everything flourishes anew because God has appeared in our midst. The Virgin Mother shows the Infant Jesus to the shepherds of Bethlehem, who rejoice and praise the Lord (cf. Lk 2:20). The Church renews the mystery for people of every generation, she shows them God's Face so that, with his blessing, they may walk on the path of peace.

This traditional meeting at the beginning of the year, two weeks after the celebration of the birth of the Incarnate Word, is a very joyful occasion for me. As we proclaimed in the liturgy: "We recognize in Christ the revelation of your love. No eye can see his glory as our God, yet now he is seen as one like us. Christ is your Son before all ages, yet now he is born in time. He has come to lift up all things to himself, to restore unity to creation" (*Preface of Christmas II*). At Christmas we contemplated the mystery of God and the mystery of creation: by the message of the angels to the shepherds, we received the good news of man's salvation and the renewal of the entire universe. That is why, in my *Message for the 2010 World Day of Peace*, I urged all persons of good will — those same men and women to whom the angels rightly promised peace — to protect creation....

The Church is open to everyone because, in God, she lives for others! She thus shares deeply in the fortunes of humanity, which in this new year continues to be marked by the dramatic crisis of the global economy and consequently a serious and widespread social instability. In my Encyclical *Caritas in Veritate*, I invited everyone to look to the deeper causes of this situation: in the last analysis, they are to be found in a current self-centered and materialistic way of thinking which fails to acknowledge the limitations inherent in every creature. Today I would like to stress that the same way of thinking also endangers creation. Each of us could probably cite an example of the damage that this has caused to the environment the world over. I will offer an example, from any number of others, taken from the recent history of Europe.

---

35 Pope Benedict XVI, Address to the Members of the Diplomatic Corps for the Traditional Exchange of New Year Greetings, January 11, 2010.

Twenty years ago, after the fall of the Berlin wall and the collapse of the materialistic and atheistic regimes which had for several decades dominated a part of this continent, was it not easy to assess the great harm which an economic system lacking any reference to the truth about man had done not only to the dignity and freedom of individuals and peoples, but to nature itself, by polluting soil, water and air? The denial of God distorts the freedom of the human person, yet it also devastates creation. It follows that the protection of creation is not principally a response to an aesthetic need, but much more to a moral need, in as much as nature expresses a plan of love and truth which is prior to us and which comes from God.

For this reason I share the growing concern caused by economic and political resistance to combating the degradation of the environment. This problem was evident even recently, during the XV Session of the Conference of the States Parties to the United Nations Framework Convention on Climate Change held in Copenhagen from December 7 to 18, 2009. I trust that in the course of this year, first in Bonn and later in Mexico City, it will be possible to reach an agreement for effectively dealing with this question. The issue is all the more important in that the very future of some nations is at stake, particularly some island states.

It is proper, however, that this concern and commitment for the environment should be situated within the larger framework of the great challenges now facing mankind. If we wish to build true peace, how can we separate, or even set at odds, the protection of the environment and the protection of human life, including the life of the unborn? It is in man's respect for himself that his sense of responsibility for creation is shown. As Saint Thomas Aquinas has taught, man represents all that is most noble in the universe (cf. *Summa Theologiae*, I, q. 29, a. 3). Furthermore, as I noted during the recent FAO World Summit on Food Security, "the world has enough food for all its inhabitants" (*Address of November 16, 2009*, No. 2) provided that selfishness does not lead some to hoard the goods which are intended for all.

I would like to stress again that the protection of creation calls for an appropriate management of the natural resources of different countries and, in the first place, of those which are economically disadvantaged. I think of the continent of Africa, which I had the joy of visiting last March during my journey to Cameroon and Angola, and which was the subject of the deliberations of the recent Special Assembly of the Synod of Bishops. The synod fathers pointed with concern to the erosion and desertification of large tracts of arable land as a result of overexploitation and environmental pollution (cf. *Propositio* 22). In Africa, as elsewhere, there is a need to make political and economic decisions which ensure "forms of agricultural and industrial production capable of respecting creation and satisfying the primary needs of all" (*Message for the 2010 World Day of Peace*, No. 10).

How can we forget, for that matter, that the struggle for access to natural resources is one of the causes of a number of conflicts, not least in Africa, as well as a continuing threat elsewhere? For this reason too, I forcefully repeat that to cultivate peace, one must protect creation! Furthermore, there are still large areas, for example in Afghanistan or in some countries of Latin America, where agriculture is unfortunately still linked to the production of narcotics, and is a not insignificant source of employment and income. If we want peace, we need to preserve creation by rechanneling these activities; I once more urge the international community not to become resigned to the drug trade and the grave moral and social problems which it creates.

Ladies and Gentlemen, the protection of creation is indeed an important element of peace and justice! Among the many challenges which it presents, one of the most serious is increased military spending and the cost of maintaining and developing nuclear arsenals. Enormous resources are being consumed for these purposes, when they could be spent on the development of peoples, especially those who are poorest. For this reason I firmly hope that, during the Nuclear Non-Proliferation Treaty Review Conference to be held this May in New York, concrete decisions will be made toward progressive disarmament, with a view to freeing our planet from nuclear arms. More generally, I deplore the fact that arms production and export helps to perpetuate conflicts and violence, as in Darfur, in Somalia, or in the Democratic Republic of the Congo.

Together with the inability of the parties directly involved to step back from the spiral of violence and pain spawned by these conflicts, there is the apparent powerlessness of other countries and the international organizations to restore peace, to say nothing of the indifference, amounting practically to resignation, of public opinion worldwide. There is no need to insist on the extent to which such conflicts damage and degrade the environment. Finally, how can I fail to mention terrorism, which endangers countless innocent lives and generates widespread anxiety. On this solemn occasion, I would like to renew the appeal which I made during the Angelus prayer of January 1, 2010, to all those belonging to armed groups, of whatever kind, to abandon the path of violence and to open their hearts to the joy of peace.

The grave acts of violence to which I have just alluded, combined with the scourges of poverty, hunger, natural disasters, and the destruction of the environment, have helped to swell the ranks of those who migrate from their native land. Given the extent of this exodus, I wish to exhort the various civil authorities to carry on their work with justice, solidarity, and foresight. Here I wish to speak in particular of the Christians of the Middle East. Beleaguered in various ways, even in the exercise of their religious freedom, they are leaving the land of their forebears, where the Church took root during the earliest centuries. To offer them encouragement and to make them feel the closeness of their brothers and sisters in faith, I have convened for next autumn a Special Assembly of the Synod of Bishops on the Middle East.

Ladies and Gentlemen, to this point I have alluded only to a few aspects of the problem of the environment. Yet the causes of the situation which is now evident to everyone are of the moral order, and the question must be faced within the framework of a great program of education aimed at promoting an effective change of thinking and at creating new lifestyles. The community of believers can and wants to take part in this, but, for it to do so, its public role must be recognized.

Sadly, in certain countries, mainly in the West, one increasingly encounters in political and cultural circles, as well in the media, scarce respect and at times hostility, if not scorn, directed toward religion and toward Christianity in particular. It is clear that if relativism is considered an essential element of democracy, one risks viewing secularity solely in the sense of excluding or, more precisely, denying the social importance of religion. But such an approach creates confrontation and division, disturbs peace, harms human ecology, and, by rejecting in principle approaches other than its own, finishes in a dead end.

There is thus an urgent need to delineate a positive and open secularity which, grounded in the just autonomy of the temporal order and the spiritual order, can foster healthy cooperation and a spirit of shared responsibility. Here I think of Europe, which, now that the Lisbon Treaty has taken effect, has entered a new phase in its process of integration, a process which the Holy See will continue to follow with close attention. Noting with satisfaction that the treaty provides for the European Union to maintain an "open, transparent and regular" dialogue with the Churches (Art. 17), I express my hope that in building its future, Europe will always draw upon the wellsprings of its Christian identity. As I said during my apostolic visit last September to the Czech Republic, Europe has an irreplaceable role to play "for the formation of the conscience of each generation and the promotion of a basic ethical consensus that serves every person who calls this continent 'home' " (*Meeting with Political and Civil Authorities and with the Diplomatic Corps*, September 26, 2009).

To carry our reflection further, we must remember that the problem of the environment is complex; one might compare it to a multifaceted prism. Creatures differ from one another and can be protected, or endangered, in different ways, as we know from daily experience. One such attack comes from laws or proposals which, in the name of fighting discrimination, strike at the biological basis of the difference between the sexes. I am thinking, for example, of certain countries in Europe or North and South America. Saint Columban stated: "If you take away freedom, you take away dignity" (*Ep. 4 ad Attela*, in *S. Columbani Opera*, Dublin, 1957, p. 34). Yet freedom cannot be absolute, since man is not himself God, but the image of God, God's creation. For man, the path to be taken cannot be determined by caprice or willfulness, but must rather correspond to the structure willed by the Creator.

The protection of creation also entails other challenges, which can only be met by international solidarity. I think of the natural disasters which this past year have sown death, suffering and destruction in the Philippines, Vietnam, Laos, Cambodia, and Taiwan. Nor can I pass over Indonesia and, closer to us, the Abruzzi region, hit by devastating earthquakes. Faced with events like these, generous aid should never be lacking, since the life itself of God's children is at stake.

Yet, in addition to solidarity, the protection of creation also calls for concord and stability between states. Whenever disagreements and conflicts arise among them, in order to defend peace they must tenaciously pursue the path of constructive dialogue. This is what happened twenty-five years ago with the Treaty of Peace and Friendship between Argentina and Chile, reached thanks to the mediation of the Apostolic See. That treaty has borne abundant fruit in cooperation and prosperity which have in some way benefited all of Latin America. In this same area of the world, I am pleased by the rapprochement upon which Columbia and Ecuador have embarked after several months of tension. Closer to us, I am gratified by the agreement concluded between Croatia and Slovenia on arbitration regarding their sea and land borders.

I am also pleased by the accord between Armenia and Turkey for the re-establishment of diplomatic relations, and I express my hope that, through dialogue, relations will improve among all the countries of the southern Caucasus. In the course of my pilgrimage to the Holy Land, I urgently appealed to the Israelis and the Palestinians to dialogue and to respect each others' rights. Once again I call for a universal recognition of the right of the State of Israel to exist and to enjoy peace and security within internationally recognized borders. Likewise, the right of the Palestinian people to a sovereign and independent homeland, to live in dignity and to enjoy freedom of movement, ought to be recognized.

I would also like to request the support of everyone for the protection of the identity and sacred character of Jerusalem, and of its cultural and religious heritage, which is of universal value. Only thus will this unique city, holy yet deeply afflicted, be a sign and harbinger of that peace which God desires for the whole human family. Out of love for the dialogue and peace which protect creation, I exhort the government leaders and the citizens of Iraq to overcome their divisions and the temptation to violence and intolerance, in order to build together the future of their country. The Christian communities also wish to make their own contribution, but if this is to happen, they need to be assured respect, security and freedom.

Pakistan has been also hard hit by violence in recent months, and certain episodes were directly aimed at the Christian minority. I ask that everything be done to avoid the reoccurrence of such acts of aggression, and to ensure that Christians feel fully a part of the life of their country. In speaking of acts of violence against Christians, I cannot fail to mention also the deplorable attack which the Egyptian Coptic community suffered in recent days, during its celebration of Christmas. Concerning Iran, I express my hope that through dialogue and cooperation joint solutions will be found on the national as well as the international level. I encourage Lebanon, which has emerged from a lengthy political crisis, to continue along the path of concord. I hope that Honduras, after a period of uncertainty and unrest, will move toward a recovery of normal political and social life. I desire the same for Guinea and Madagascar with the effective and disinterested aid of the international community.

Ladies and Gentlemen, at the end of this rapid overview which, due to its brevity, cannot mention every situation worthy of note, I am reminded of the words of the apostle Paul, for whom "all creation groans and is in agony" and "we ourselves groan inwardly" (Rom 8:20-23). There is so much suffering in our world, and human selfishness continues in many ways to harm creation. For this reason, the yearning for salvation which affects all creation is that much more intense and present in the hearts of all men and women, believers and nonbelievers alike. The Church points out that the response to this aspiration is Christ "the firstborn of all creation, for in him all things in heaven and on earth were created" (Col 1:15-16). Looking to him, I exhort every person of good will to work confidently and generously for the sake of human dignity and freedom.

May the light and strength of Jesus help us to respect human ecology, in the knowledge that natural ecology will likewise benefit, since the book of nature is one and indivisible. In this way we will be able to build peace, today and for the sake of generations to come. To all I wish a Happy New Year!

THE MYSTERIES OF NATURE[36]

The quest for the sacred does not devalue other fields of human enquiry. On the contrary, it places them in a context which magnifies their importance, as ways of responsibly exercising our stewardship over creation. In the Bible, we read that, after the work of creation was completed, God blessed our first parents and said to them, "Be fruitful and multiply, and fill the earth and subdue it" (Gn 1:28). He entrusted us with the task of exploring and harnessing the mysteries of nature in order to serve a higher good. What is that higher good? In the Christian faith, it is expressed as love for God and love for our neighbor. And so we engage with the world wholeheartedly and enthusiastically, but always with a view to serving that higher good, lest we disfigure the beauty of creation by exploiting it for selfish purposes.

So it is that genuine religious belief points us beyond present utility toward the transcendent. It reminds us of the possibility and the imperative of moral conversion, of the duty to live peaceably with our neighbor, of the importance of living a life of integrity. Properly understood, it brings enlightenment, it purifies our hearts, and it inspires noble and generous action, to the benefit of the entire human family. It motivates us to cultivate the practice of virtue and to reach out toward one another in love, with the greatest respect for religious traditions different from our own.

---

36 Pope Benedict XVI, Address, September 17, 2010.

God's Gift of Creation[37]

The proclamation of the word of God and the protection of creation

Engagement with the world, as demanded by God's word, makes us look with new eyes at the entire created cosmos, which contains traces of that word through whom all things were made (cf. Jn 1:2). As men and women who believe in and proclaim the Gospel, we have a responsibility toward creation. Revelation makes known God's plan for the cosmos, yet it also leads us to denounce that mistaken attitude which refuses to view all created realities as a reflection of their Creator, but instead as mere raw material, to be exploited without scruple. Man thus lacks that essential humility which would enable him to see creation as a gift from God, to be received and used in accordance with his plan. Instead, the arrogance of human beings who live "as if God did not exist" leads them to exploit and disfigure nature, failing to see it as the handiwork of the creative word. In this theological context, I would like to echo the statements of the synod fathers who reminded us that "accepting the word of God, attested to by Scripture and by the Church's living Tradition, gives rise to a new way of seeing things, promotes an authentic ecology which has its deepest roots in the obedience of faith ... [and] develops a renewed theological sensitivity to the goodness of all things, which are created in Christ" (*Propositio* 54). We need to be re-educated in wonder and in the ability to recognize the beauty made manifest in created realities (cf. Benedict XVI, *Sacramentum Caritatis*, No. 92).

---

37   Pope Benedict XVI, Apostolic Exhortation *Verbum Domini*, September 30, 2010.

1. The annual celebration of World Food Day is an occasion to draw up a balance sheet of all that has been achieved through the commitment of the Food and Agriculture Organization of the United Nations (FAO) to guarantee daily food for millions of our brothers and sisters throughout the world. It also provides a suitable occasion to note the difficulties that are encountered when the necessary attitudes of solidarity are lacking.

Too often, attention is diverted from the needs of populations, insufficient emphasis is placed on work in the fields, and the goods of the earth are not given adequate protection. As a result, economic imbalance is produced, and the inalienable rights and dignity of every human person are ignored.

The theme of this year's World Food Day, *United against Hunger*, is a timely reminder that everyone needs to make a commitment to give the agricultural sector its proper importance. Everyone — from individuals to the organizations of civil society, states, and international institutions — needs to give priority to one of the most urgent goals for the human family: freedom from hunger. In order to achieve freedom from hunger it is necessary to ensure not only that enough food is available, but also that everyone has daily access to it: this means promoting whatever resources and infrastructures are necessary in order to sustain production and distribution on a scale sufficient to guarantee fully the right to food.

The efforts to achieve this goal will surely help to build up the unity of the human family throughout the world. Concrete initiatives are needed, informed by charity, and inspired by truth — initiatives that are capable of overcoming natural obstacles

---

38 Pope Benedict XVI, Message to Mr. Jacques Diouf, Director General of FAO on the Occasion of World Food Day, October 15, 2010.

linked to the cycles of the seasons or to environmental conditions, as well as man-made obstacles. Charity, practiced in the light of truth, can bring an end to divisions and conflicts so as to allow the goods of the earth to pass between peoples in a lively and continuous exchange.

An important step forward was the international community's recent decision to protect the right to water which, as FAO has always maintained, is essential to human nutrition, to rural activities, and to the conservation of nature. Indeed, as my venerable predecessor Pope John Paul II observed in his *Message for the 2002 World Food Day*, many different religions and cultures recognize a symbolic value in water, from which there "springs an invitation to be fully aware of the importance of this precious commodity, and consequently to revise present patterns of behavior in order to guarantee, today and in the future, that all people shall have access to the water indispensable for their needs, and that productive activities, and agriculture in particular, shall enjoy adequate levels of this priceless resource" (*Message for the 2002 World Food Day*, October 13, 2002).

2. If the international community is to be truly "united" against hunger, then poverty must be overcome through *authentic human development*, based on the idea of the person as a unity of body, soul, and spirit. Today, though, there is a tendency to limit the vision of development to one that satisfies the material needs of the person, especially through access to technology; yet authentic development is not simply a function of what a person "has," it must also embrace higher values of fraternity, solidarity, and the common good.

Amid the pressures of globalization, under the influence of interests that often remain fragmented, it is wise to propose a model of development built on *fraternity*: if it is inspired by solidarity and directed toward the common good, it will be able to provide correctives to the current global crisis. In order to sustain levels of food security in the short term, adequate funding must be provided so as to make it possible for agriculture to reactivate production cycles, despite the deterioration of climatic and environmental conditions. These conditions, it must be said, have a markedly negative impact on rural populations, crop systems, and working patterns, especially in countries that are already afflicted with food shortages. Developed countries have to be aware that the world's growing needs require consistent levels of aid from them. They cannot simply remain closed towards others: such an attitude would not help to resolve the crisis.

In this context, FAO has the essential task of examining the issue of world hunger at the institutional level and proposing particular initiatives that involve its member states in responding to the growing demand for food. Indeed, the nations of the world are called to give and to receive in proportion to their effective needs, by reason of that "*pressing moral need for renewed solidarity*, especially in relationships between developing countries and those that are highly industrialized" (*Caritas in Veritate*, No. 49).

3. The recent worthy campaign " *1 Billion Hungry,*" by which FAO seeks to raise awareness of the urgency of the fight against hunger, has highlighted the need for an adequate response both from individual countries and from the international community, even when the response is limited to assistance or emergency aid. This is why a reform of international institutions according to the principle of subsidiarity is essential, since "institutions by themselves are not enough, because integral human development is primarily a vocation, and therefore it involves a free assumption of responsibility in solidarity on the part of everyone" (*ibid.,* No. 11).

In order to eliminate hunger and malnutrition, obstacles of self-interest must be overcome so as to make room for a fruitful *gratuitousness,* manifested in international cooperation as an expression of genuine fraternity. This does not obviate the need for justice, though, and it is important that existing rules be respected and implemented, in addition to whatever plans for intervention and programs of action may prove necessary. Individuals, peoples, and countries must be allowed to shape their own development, taking advantage of external assistance in accordance with priorities and concepts rooted in their traditional techniques, in their culture, in their religious patrimony and in the wisdom passed on from generation to generation within the family.

Invoking the blessing of the Almighty upon the activities of FAO, I wish to assure you, Mr. Director General, that the Church is always ready to work for the defeat of hunger. Indeed, she is constantly at work, through her own structures, to alleviate the poverty and deprivation afflicting large parts of the world's population, and she is fully conscious that her own engagement in this field forms part of a common international effort to promote unity and peace among the community of peoples.

The history of science in the twentieth century is one of undoubted achievement and major advances. Unfortunately, the popular image of twentieth-century science is sometimes characterized otherwise, in two extreme ways. On the one hand, science is posited by some as a panacea, proven by its notable achievements in the last century. Its innumerable advances were in fact so encompassing and so rapid that they seemed to confirm the point of view that science might answer all the questions of man's existence, and even of his highest aspirations. On the other hand, there are those who fear science and who distance themselves from it, because of sobering developments such as the construction and terrifying use of nuclear weapons.

Science, of course, is not defined by either of these extremes. Its task was and remains a patient yet passionate search for the truth about the cosmos, about nature, and about the constitution of the human being.

In this search, there have been many successes and failures, triumphs and setbacks. The developments of science have been both uplifting, as when the complexity of nature and its phenomena were discovered, exceeding our expectations, and humbling, as when some of the theories we thought might have explained those phenomena once and for all proved only partial. Nonetheless, even provisional results constitute a real contribution to unveiling the correspondence between the intellect and natural realities, on which later generations may build further.

The progress made in scientific knowledge in the twentieth century, in all its various disciplines, has led to a greatly improved awareness of the place that man and this planet occupy in the universe. In all sciences, the common denominator continues to

---

39 Pope Benedict XVI, Address to the Participants in the 2010 Plenary Session of the Pontifical Academy of Sciences, October 28, 2010.

be the notion of experimentation as an organized method for observing nature.

In the last century, man certainly made more progress — if not always in his knowledge of himself and of God, then certainly in his knowledge of the macro- and microcosms — than in the entire previous history of humanity. Our meeting here today, dear friends, is a proof of the Church's esteem for ongoing scientific research and of her gratitude for scientific endeavor, which she both encourages and benefits from. In our own day, scientists themselves appreciate more and more the need to be open to philosophy if they are to discover the logical and epistemological foundation for their methodology and their conclusions.

For her part, the Church is convinced that scientific activity ultimately benefits from the recognition of man's spiritual dimension and his quest for ultimate answers that allow for the acknowledgement of a world existing independently from us, which we do not fully understand and which we can only comprehend insofar as we grasp its inherent logic. Scientists do not create the world; they learn about it and attempt to imitate it, following the laws and intelligibility that nature manifests to us.

The scientist's experience as a human being is therefore that of perceiving a constant, a law, a logos that he has not created but that he has instead observed: in fact, it leads us to admit the existence of an all-powerful Reason, which is other than that of man, and which sustains the world. This is the meeting point between the natural sciences and religion. As a result, science becomes a place of dialogue, a meeting between man and nature and, potentially, even between man and his Creator.

As we look to the twenty-first century, I would like to propose two thoughts for further reflection. First, as increasing accomplishments of the sciences deepen our wonder of the complexity of nature, the need for an interdisciplinary approach tied with philosophical reflection leading to a synthesis is more and more perceived. Secondly, scientific achievement in this new century should always be informed by the imperatives of fraternity and peace, helping to solve the great problems of humanity, and directing everyone's efforts toward the true good of man and the integral development of the peoples of the world. The positive outcome of twenty-first-century science will surely depend in large measure on the scientist's ability to search for truth and apply discoveries in a way that goes hand in hand with the search for what is just and good.

With these sentiments, I invite you to direct your gaze toward Christ, the uncreated Wisdom, and to recognize in His face, the Logos of the Creator of all things. Renewing my good wishes for your work, I willingly impart my apostolic blessing.

In the second reading of today's liturgy, the apostle Paul underlines the importance of work for the life of man. We are reminded of this idea on "Thanksgiving Day," that is traditionally celebrated in Italy on this second Sunday in November, as the offering of thanks to God at the end of the harvest season. Although in other geographical areas farming periods naturally differ, today I would like to draw inspiration from St. Paul's words to reflect on agricultural work in particular.

The full gravity of the current economic crisis, discussed these past few days at the G20 Summit, should be understood. This crisis has numerous causes and is a strong reminder of the need for a profound revision of the model of global economic development (*cf.* Encyclical *Caritas in Veritate*, No. 21).

It is an acute symptom which has been added to a long list of many far more serious and well-known problems, such as the lasting imbalance between wealth and poverty, the scandal of world hunger, the ecological emergency, and the now widespread problem of unemployment.

In this context, a strategic revitalization of agriculture is crucial. Indeed, the process of industrialization has often overshadowed the agricultural sector, which, although benefiting in its turn from modern technology, has nevertheless lost importance with notable consequences, even at the cultural level. It seems to me that it is time to re-evaluate agriculture, not in a nostalgic sense but as an indispensable resource for the future.

In the present economic situation, the dynamic economies are tempted to pursue advantageous alliances, which nevertheless may have detrimental results for other poorer states, situations of extreme poverty among the masses, and the depletion of the

---

40   Pope Benedict XVI, Angelus, November 14, 2010.

natural resources of the earth that God has entrusted to man, as it says in Genesis, so that he may till it and keep it (*cf.* 2:15). And in spite of the crisis it can still be seen that in the old industrialized countries lifestyles marked by unsustainable consumerism are encouraged. These also prove damaging for the environment and for the poor. Then a really concerted aim for a new balance between farming, industry, and services is necessary so that development may be sustainable, so that no one will lack bread and work, air and water, and that the other fundamental resources may be preserved as universal rights (*cf. Caritas in Veritate*, No. 27).

Thus it is essential to cultivate and spread a clear ethical awareness that is equal to facing the most complicated challenges of our time. Everyone should be taught to consume in a wiser and more responsible way. We should promote personal responsibility along with a social dimension of rural activities based on the undying values of hospitality, solidarity, and sharing the toil of labor. Many young people have already chosen this path, and many professionals are also returning to agricultural enterprises, feeling that in this way they are not only responding to personal and family needs, but also to a *sign of the times,* to a concrete sensibility for the *common good.*

Let us pray to the Virgin Mary that these reflections may serve as an incentive to the international community, as we thank God for the fruits of the earth and the work of mankind.

THE GOAL OF AN "ECOLOGY OF THE HUMAN PERSON"[41]

21. The goal of the Church's entire educational commitment is easily identified, namely, working to construct what Pope Benedict XVI calls an "ecology of the human person." "There is need for what might be called a human ecology, correctly understood. [...] The decisive issue is the overall moral tenor of society. If there is a lack of respect for the right to life and to a natural death, if human conception, gestation, and birth are made artificial, if human embryos are sacrificed to research, the conscience of society ends up losing the concept of human ecology and, along with it, that of environmental ecology. It is contradictory to insist that future generations respect the natural environment when our educational systems and laws do not help them to respect themselves. The book of nature is one and indivisible: it takes in not only the environment, but also life, sexuality, marriage, the family, social relations: in a word, integral human development. Our duties toward the environment are linked to our duties toward the human person, considered in himself and in relation to others. It would be wrong to uphold one set of duties while trampling on the other. Herein lies a grave contradiction in our mentality and practice today: one which demeans the person, disrupts the environment and damages society" (Benedict XVI, *Caritas in Veritate,* No. 51).

The Christian faith assists the intelligence in understanding the profound underlying equilibrium of history and all existence. It accomplishes this not in a general or external way but by sharing with reason a thirst for knowledge and inquiry, directing reason toward the well-being of man and the cosmos. The Christian

41 Synod of Bishops, XIII Ordinary General Assembly, The New Evangelization for the Transmission of the Christian Faith, *Lineamenta*, February 2, 2011.

faith helps us understand the profound content of basic human experiences, as the above text shows. This critical and focused discussion has been the work of Catholicism for a long time. The Church becomes increasingly better equipped in this work by establishing institutions, centers of research, and universities, which are the fruit of the intuition and charisms of some institutes or of the concern of local churches for education. These institutions fulfill their role in collaborative efforts in research and the development of knowledge in various cultures and societies. The social and cultural changes presented thus far are raising questions and posing challenges to these institutions. Because of her commitment to education and culture, the Church is called to undertake a process of discernment, which is the first step in the "new evangelization," so as to be able to distinguish the critical aspects of these challenges and forces and adopt the strategies which will be a guarantee in the future of not only the Church, but also the individual and humanity.

Surely, a "new evangelization" considers these areas of culture as "Courtyards of the Gentiles," helping them live up to their basic purpose or "vocation" in the changes they are experiencing, namely, bringing the question of God and the Christian faith to the conversations of our times and making these areas a place where persons can be formed to be free and mature and, in turn, capable of bringing the question of God into their own lives, families, and workplace.

Talk with the Astronauts in Orbit[42]

Introduction

Dear Astronauts,

I am very happy to have this extraordinary opportunity to converse with you during your mission. I am especially grateful to be able to speak to so many of you, as both crews are present on the space station at this time.

Humanity is experiencing a period of extremely rapid progress in the fields of scientific knowledge and technical applications. In a sense, you are our representatives — spearheading humanity's exploration of new spaces and possibilities for our future, going beyond the limitations of our everyday existence.

We all admire your courage, as well as the discipline and commitment with which you prepared yourselves for this mission. We are convinced you are inspired by noble ideals and that you intend placing the results of your research and endeavors at the disposal of all humanity and for the common good.

This conversation gives me the chance to express my own admiration and appreciation to you and to all those who collaborate in making your mission possible, and to add my heartfelt encouragement to bring it to a safe and successful conclusion.

But this is a conversation, so I must not be the only one doing the talking.

I am very curious to hear you tell me about your experiences and your reflections.

If you don't mind, I would like to ask you a few questions …

---

42 Pope Benedict XVI Talk with the Astronauts in Orbit Via Satellite Connection with the Crew of the International Space Station, May 21, 2011.

FIRST QUESTION

From the space station you have a very different view of the Earth. You fly over different continents and nations several times a day. I think it must be obvious to you how we all live together on one Earth and how absurd it is that we fight and kill each other. I know that Mark Kelly's wife was a victim of a serious attack, and I hope her health continues to improve. When you are contemplating the Earth from up there, do you ever wonder about the way nations and people live together down here, or about how science can contribute to the cause of peace?

MARK KELLY, USA:

Well, thank you for the kind words, Your Holiness, and thank you for mentioning my wife, Gabby. It's a very good question: we fly over most of the world and you don't see borders, but at the same time we realize that people fight with each other and there is a lot of violence in this world, and it's really an unfortunate thing. Usually, people fight over many different things. As we've seen in the Middle East right now: it's somewhat for democracy in certain areas, but usually people fight for resources. And it's interesting in space … on Earth, people often fight for energy; in space we use solar power, and we have fuel cells on the space station. You know, the science and the technology that we put into the space station to develop a solar-power capability, gives us pretty much an unlimited amount of energy. And if those technologies could be adapted more on Earth, we could possibly reduce some of that violence.

SECOND QUESTION

One of the themes I often return to in my discourses concerns the responsibility we all have toward the future of our planet. I recall the serious risks facing the environment and the survival of future generations. Scientists tell us we have to be careful and from an ethical point of view we must develop our consciences as well.

From your extraordinary observation point, how do you see the situation on Earth?

Do you see signs or phenomena to which we need to be more attentive?

Ron Garan, USA:

Well, Your Holiness, it's a great honor to speak with you, and you're right: it really is an extraordinary vantage point we have up here. On the one hand, we can see how indescribably beautiful the planet that we have been given is; but on the other hand, we can really clearly see how fragile it is. Just the atmosphere, for instance: the atmosphere when viewed from space is paper-thin, and to think that this paper-thin layer is all that separates every living thing from the vacuum of space and is all that protects us, is really a sobering thought. You know, it seems to us that it's just incredible to view the Earth hanging in the blackness of space and to think that we are all on this together, riding through this beautiful fragile oasis through the universe; it really fills us with a lot of hope to think that all of us on board this incredible orbiting space station that was built by the many nations of our international partnership, to accomplish this tremendous feat in orbit, I think ... you know, that just shows that by working together and by cooperating we can overcome many of the problems that face our planet; we could solve many of the challenges that face the inhabitants of our planet ... it really is a wonderful place to live and work, and it's a wonderful place to view our beautiful Earth.

THIRD QUESTION

The experience you are having right now is both extraordinary and very important — even if you must eventually come back down to Earth like all the rest of us.

When you do return, you will be much admired and treated like heroes who speak and act with authority. You will be asked to talk about your experiences. What will be the most important messages you would like to convey — to young people especially — who will live in a world strongly influenced by your experiences and discoveries?

MIKE FINCHKE, USA:

Your Holiness, as my colleagues have indicated, we can look down and see our beautiful planet Earth that God has made, and it is the most beautiful planet in the whole solar system. However, if we look up, we can see the rest of the universe, and the rest of the universe is out there for us to go explore. And the International Space Station is just one symbol, one example of what human beings can do when we work together constructively. So our message, I think — one of our many messages, but I think one of our most important messages — is to let the children of the planet know, the young people know that there is a whole universe for us to go explore. And when we do it together, there is nothing that we cannot accomplish.

FOURTH QUESTION

Space exploration is a fascinating scientific adventure. I know that you have been installing new equipment to further scientific research and the study of radiation coming from outer space. But I think it is also an adventure of the human spirit, a powerful stimulus to reflect on the origins and on the destiny of the universe and humanity. Believers often look up at the limitless heavens and, meditating on the Creator of it all, they are struck by the mystery of his greatness. That is why the medal I gave Robert (Vittori), as a sign of my own participation in your mission, represents the Creation of Man — as painted by Michelangelo on the Sistine Chapel ceiling. In the midst of your intense work and research, do you ever stop and reflect like this — perhaps even to say a prayer to the Creator? Or will it be easier for you to think about these things once you have returned to Earth?

ROBERTO VITTORI, ITALY:

Your Holiness, to live on board the International Space Station, to work as an astronaut on the shuttle Soyuz of the station, is extremely intense. But we all have an opportunity, when the nights come, to look down on Earth: our planet, the blue planet, is beautiful. Blue is the color of our planet, blue is the color of the sky, blue is also the color of the Italian Air Force, the organization that gave me the opportunity to then join the Italian Space Agency and the European Space Agency. When we have a moment to look down, beauty which is the three-dimensional effect of the beauty of the planet is capturing our heart, is capturing my heart. And I do pray: I do pray for me, for our families, for our future. I took with me the coin, and I allow this coin to float in front of me to demonstrate lack of gravity. I shall thank you very much for this opportunity, and I'd like to allow this coin to float to my friend and colleague Paolo: he will make return to Earth on the Soyuz. I brought it with me to space, and he will take it down to Earth to then give it back to you.

Final greeting

Dear Astronauts,

I thank you warmly for this wonderful opportunity to meet and dialogue with you. You have helped me and many other people to reflect together on important issues that regard the future of humanity. I wish you the very best for your work and for the success of your great mission at the service of science, international collaboration, authentic progress, and for peace in the world. I will continue to follow you in my thoughts and prayers, and I willingly impart my apostolic blessing.

THE GREAT HALLEL PSALM 136 (135)

I would like to meditate with you on a Psalm that sums up the entire history of salvation recorded in the Old Testament. It is a great hymn of praise that celebrates the Lord in the multiple, repeated expressions of his goodness throughout human history: it is Psalm 136, or 135 according to the Greco-Latin tradition.

A solemn prayer of thanksgiving, known as the "Great Hallel," this Psalm is traditionally sung at the end of the Jewish Passover meal and was probably also prayed by Jesus at the Last Supper celebrated with his disciples. In fact, the annotation of the Evangelists, "and when they had sung a hymn, they went out to the Mount of Olives" (cf. Mt 26:30; Mk 14:26), would seem to allude to it.

The horizon of praise thus appears to illumine the difficult path to Golgotha. The whole of Psalm 136 unfolds in the form of a litany, marked by the antiphonal refrain: "for his steadfast love endures for ever." The many wonders God has worked in human history and his continuous intervention on behalf of his people are listed in the composition. Furthermore, to every proclamation of the Lord's saving action the antiphon responds with the basic impetus of praise.

The eternal love of God is a love which, in accordance with the Hebrew term used, suggestive of fidelity, mercy, kindness, grace, and tenderness, is the unifying motif of the entire Psalm. The refrain always takes the same form, whereas the regular paradigmatic manifestations of God's love change: creation, liberation through the Exodus, the gift of land, the Lord's provident and constant help for his people and for every created being.

---

43 Pope Benedict XVI, General Audience, October 19, 2011.

After a triple invitation to give thanks to God as sovereign (vv. 1-3), the Lord is celebrated as the One who works "great wonders" (v. 4), the first of which is the Creation: the heavens, the earth, the heavenly bodies (vv. 5-9). The created world is not merely a scenario into which God's saving action is inserted, rather is the very beginning of that marvelous action. With the Creation, the Lord shows himself in all his goodness and beauty, he commits himself to life, revealing a desire for goodness which gives rise to every other action of salvation.

And in our Psalm, re-echoing the first chapter of Genesis, the principal elements of the created world are summed up, with special insistence on the heavenly bodies, the sun, the moon, and the stars, magnificent created things that govern the day and the night. Nothing is said here of the creation of human beings, but they are ever present; the sun and the moon are for them — for men and women — so as to structure human time, setting it in relation to the Creator, especially by denoting the liturgical seasons. And it is precisely the feast of Easter that is immediately evoked when, passing to God's manifestation of himself in history, the great event of the exodus, freedom from slavery in Egypt, begins, whose most significant elements are outlined:

... At the Red Sea too the Lord acted with merciful power. Before an Israel so terrified by the sight of the Egyptians in pursuit as to regret its departure from Egypt (cf. Ex 14:10-12), God, as our Psalm says, "divided the Red Sea in sunder ... and made the people of Israel pass through the midst of it ... but overthrew Pharaoh and his host" (vv. 13-15). The image of the Red Sea "divided" into two seems to call to mind the idea of the sea as a great monster hacked into two and thereby rendered harmless. The might of the Lord overcomes the danger of the forces of nature and of these soldiers deployed in battle array by men: the sea, which seemed to bar the way of the People of God, let Israel cross on dry ground and then swept over the Egyptians, submerging them. Thus the full salvific force of the Lord's "mighty hand, and an outstretched arm" (cf. Dt 5:15; 7:19; 26:8) was demonstrated: the unjust oppressor was vanquished, engulfed by the waters, while the people of God "walked on dry ground through the sea," continuing its journey to freedom.

Our Psalm now refers to this journey, recalling in one short phrase Israel's long pilgrimage toward the promised land: he "led his people through the wilderness, for his steadfast love endures for ever" (v. 16). These few words refer to a forty-year experience, a crucial period for Israel, which in letting itself be guided by the Lord learned to live in faith, obedience, and docility to God's law. These were difficult years, marked by hardship in the desert, but also happy years, trusting in the Lord with filial trust. It was the time of "youth," as the Prophet Jeremiah describes it in speaking to Israel in the Lord's name with words full of tenderness and nostalgia: "I remember the devotion of your youth, your love as a bride, how you followed me in the wilderness, in a land not sown" (Jer 2:2).

… So as the "great wonders" that our Psalm lists unfold, we reach the moment of the conclusive gift, the fulfillment of the divine promise made to the Fathers: "gave their land as a heritage, for his steadfast love endures for ever; a heritage to Israel his servant, for his steadfast love endures for ever" (vv. 21-22). Then, in celebrating the Lord's eternal love, the gift of land was commemorated, a gift that the people were to receive but without ever taking possession of it, continuing to live in an attitude of grateful acknowledgment and gratitude.

Israel received the land it was to live in as "a heritage," a generic term which designates the possession of a good received from another person, a right of ownership which specifically refers to the paternal patrimony. One of God's prerogatives is "giving," and now, at the end of the journey of the Exodus, Israel, the recipient of the gift, enters as a son or daughter the land of the promise now fulfilled. The time of wandering, of living in tents, of living a precarious life, is over.

It was then that the happy period of permanence began, of joy in building houses, of planting vineyards, of living in security (cf. Dt 8:7-13). Yet it was also the time of the temptation to idolatry, contamination with pagans, self-sufficiency that led to the origin of the gift being forgotten.

… At this point a question arises: how can we make this Psalm our own prayer, how can we ourselves claim this Psalm as our own prayer? What is important is the Psalm's setting, for at the beginning and at the end is the Creation. Let us return to this point: the Creation as God's great gift by which we live and in which he reveals himself in his great goodness. Therefore, to think of the Creation as a gift of God is a common point for all of us.

The history of salvation then follows. We can, of course, say: this liberation from Egypt, the time in the desert, the entry into the Holy Land, and all the other subsequent problems are very remote from us, they are not part of our own history. Yet we must be attentive to the fundamental structure of this prayer. The basic structure is that Israel remembers the Lord's goodness. In this history, dark valleys, arduous journeys and death succeed one another, but Israel recalls that God was good and can survive in this dark valley, in this valley of death, because it remembers. It remembers the Lord's goodness and his power; his mercy is effective for ever. And this is also important for us: to remember the Lord's goodness. Memory strongly sustains hope. Memory tells us: God exists, God is good, his mercy endures for ever. So it is that memory unfolds, even in the darkest day or time, showing the way toward the future. It represents "great lights" and is our guiding star. We too have good memories of the goodness, of God's merciful love that endures for ever.

… We must truly treasure this story, and in order to trust must keep ever present in our mind the memory of the great things he has also worked in my life: his mercy endures for ever. And if today I am immersed in the dark night, tomorrow he sets me free, for his mercy is eternal.

Let us return to the Psalm, because at the end it returns to the Creation. The Lord, it says, "gives food to all flesh, for his steadfast love endures for ever" (v. 25). The prayer of the Psalm concludes with an invitation to praise: "Give thanks to the God of heaven, for his steadfast love endures for ever."

The Lord is our good and provident Father, who gives his children their heritage and lavishes life-giving food upon all. God who created the heavens and the earth and the great heavenly bodies, who entered human history to bring all his children to salvation is the God who fills the universe with his presence of goodness, caring for life, and providing bread.

The invisible power of the Creator and Lord of which the Psalm sings is revealed in the humble sign of the bread he gives us, with which he enables us to live. And so it is that this daily bread symbolizes and sums up the love of God as Father and opens us to the fulfillment of the New Testament, to that "Bread of Life," the Eucharist, which accompanies us in our lives as believers, anticipating the definitive joy of the messianic banquet in heaven.

Brothers and Sisters, the praise and blessing of Psalm 136[135], has made us review the most important stages in the history of salvation, to reach the Paschal Mystery in which God's saving action reaches its culmination. Let us therefore celebrate with grateful joy the Creator, Savior and faithful Father, who "so loved the world that he gave his only Son, that whoever believes in him should not perish but have eternal life" (Jn 3:16). In the fullness of time, the Son of God became man to give life, for the salvation of each one of us, and gave himself as bread in the Eucharistic mystery to enable us to enter his covenant which makes us his children. May both God's merciful goodness and his sublime "steadfast love forever" reach far afield.

I would therefore like to conclude this catechesis by making my own the words that St. John wrote in his first letter and that we must always have in mind in our prayers: "See what love the Father has given us, that we should be called children of God; and so we are" (1 Jn 3:1). Many thanks.

RESPECT FOR CREATION AND THE ECOSYSTEM[44]

79. Together with the synod fathers, I ask all the members of the Church to work and speak out in favor of an economy that cares for the poor and is resolutely opposed to an unjust order which, under the pretext of reducing poverty, has often helped to aggravate it (cf. *Propositiones* 17 and 29). God has given Africa important natural resources. Given the chronic poverty of its people, who suffer the effects of exploitation and embezzlement of funds both locally and abroad, the opulence of certain groups shocks the human conscience. Organized for the creation of wealth in their homelands, and not infrequently with the complicity of those in power in Africa, these groups too often ensure their own prosperity at the expense of the well-being of the local population (cf. *Final Message*, No. 32). Acting in concert with all other components of civil society, the Church must speak out against the unjust order that prevents the peoples of Africa from consolidating their economies (cf. Benedict XVI, *Caritas in Veritate*, No. 42) and "from developing according to their cultural characteristics" (Second Ordinary General Assembly of the Synod of Bishops, Document *Justitia in Mundo*, November 30, 1971). Moreover, it is incumbent upon the Church to strive that "every people may be the principal agent of its own economic and social progress …and may help to bring about the universal common good as an active and responsible member of the human family, on an equal footing with other peoples" (*Ibid.*, *Propositions* 8b and 8c).

80. Some businessmen and women, governments, and financial groups are involved in programs of exploitation which pollute the environment and cause unprecedented desertifica-

---

44 Pope Benedict XVI, Address to Bishops of Benin, November 19, 2011.

tion. Serious damage is done to nature, to the forests, to flora and fauna, and countless species risk extinction. All of this threatens the entire ecosystem and consequently the survival of humanity (cf. *Propositio* 22). I call upon the Church in Africa to encourage political leaders to protect such fundamental goods as land and water for the human life of present and future generations (cf. *Propositio* 30) and for peace between peoples.

Lord Cardinal, Distinguished Authorities, Dear Youngsters and Youths!

It is with great joy that I welcome all of you to this meeting dedicated to commitment to "Sister Nature," to use the name of the foundation that organized it.

I cordially greet Cardinal Rodríguez Maradiaga, and I thank him for the words he also addressed to me in your name and for the gift of the beautiful reproduction of Codex 338, which contains the oldest Franciscan sources. I greet the president, Mr. Roberto Leoni, as well as the authorities and personalities and the numerous teachers and parents. But above all I greet you, youth, dear young people! It is precisely for you that I wanted this meeting, and I would like to tell you that I appreciate very much your choice to be "guardians of creation," and in this you have my full support.

First of all we must remember that your foundation and this same meeting have a deep Franciscan inspiration. Even today's date was chosen to commemorate the proclamation of Saint Francis of Assisi, patron saint of ecology, by my beloved predecessor, Blessed John Paul II in 1979. You all know that Saint Francis is also a patron of Italy. But perhaps you do not know that he was so declared by Pope Pius XII, in 1939, who called him "the most Italian of the saints, the holiest of the Italians." If, therefore, the patron saint of Italy is also the patron of ecology, it seems fitting that young Italians should have a special feeling for "sister nature," and concretely work to defend her.

When studying Italian literature, one of the earliest texts found in the anthologies is in fact Saint Francis of Assisi's "Canticle of Brother Sun," or "of creatures": "Most high, all powerful,

---

45 Pope Benedict XVI to Students Participating in *Sorella natura*, November 28, 2011.

all good Lord! ...." This song highlights the right place to give to the Creator, the One who has called into existence all the great symphony of creatures. "All praise is yours, all glory, all honor, and all blessing. To you, alone, Most High, do they belong. Be praised, my Lord, through all your creatures." These verses are part of your educational and cultural tradition. But first they are a prayer, that educates the heart in dialogue with God, teaches it to see the imprint of the great heavenly Artist on all creatures, as we read in the beautiful Psalm 19: "The heavens declare the glory of God, the firmament proclaims the works of his hands.... There is no speech, no words; their voice is not heard; A report goes forth through all the earth, their messages, to the ends of the world"(vv. 4-5). Brother Francis, faithful to Sacred Scripture, invites us to recognize in nature a wonderful book that speaks to us of God, its beauty and goodness. It is enough to think of the fact that the Poverello of Assisi always asked the monk in charge of the garden of the convent not to cultivate all the land for vegetables, but leave some for flowers, moreover to cultivate a beautiful bed of flowers, so that the people who passed by would raise their thoughts to God, the creator of such beauty (cf. *Vita*, Thomas of Celano, CXXIV, 165).

Dear friends, the Church, noting with appreciation the most important research and scientific discoveries, has never ceased to recall that respect for the Creator's imprint in all creation leads to a better understanding of our true and deepest human identity. If properly undertaken, this respect can help a young person to also discover talents and personal ability, and therefore help prepare them for a certain profession, which they will always try to perform in full respect for the environment. In fact, if in his work, man forgets he is God's collaborator, then he can cause violence to creation, which always has a negative impact on humans, as we have seen, unfortunately, on several occasions. Today more than ever, it has become clear that respect for the environment cannot leave aside the recognition of the value of the human person and its inviolability at every stage and in every condition of life. Respect for the human being and respect for nature are one, but both can grow and find their right measure if we respect in the human being and in nature the Creator and his creation. On this, dear young people, I believe to find allies in you, true "guardians of life and creation."

And now I would like to take this opportunity to say some words to the teachers and authorities who are present here. I would emphasize the great importance of education in this field of ecology. I gladly accepted the proposal of this meeting because it involves so many young students, because it has a clear educational perspective. And, in fact, it has become apparent that there will be no good future for humanity on earth if we do not educate everyone to a more responsible way of life for creation. And this style is learned first at home and in school. I encourage you, therefore, parents, school administrators, and teachers to carry on with a constant commitment to education and teaching focus for this purpose. Moreover, it is essential that institutions in charge, who are well represented here today, support this work of families and schools.

Dear friends, we entrust these thoughts and aspirations to the Virgin Mary, Mother of all humanity. As we have just entered the season of Advent, may she accompany us and lead us to recognize in Christ the center of the universe, the light that enlightens every man and every creature. And Saint Francis teach us to sing with all creation a hymn of praise and thanksgiving to our heavenly Father, giver of every gift. Thank you so much for coming, and I willingly accompany your study, your work, and your commitment with my blessing. I spoke of singing; let us sing together the Our Father, the great prayer taught to us all by Jesus.

Books by Pope Benedict XVI
from Our Sunday Visitor

The Apostles

The Fathers, Volume I
St. Clement to St. Augustine

The Fathers, Volume II
St. Leo to St. Bernard

The Apostles, Illustrated

The Fathers, Illustrated
Volume I — St. Clement to St. Paulinus of Nola
Volume II — St. Augustine to St. Maximus the Confessor

Breakfast with Benedict

Questions and Answers

Saint Paul the Apostle

The Virtues

Great Teachers

Holy Women

Doctors of the Church

The Priest, A Bridge to God

Our Sunday Visitor Publishing
1-800-348-2440 ◆ www.osv.com